HOW DOES GOD USE SUFFERING FOR OUR GOOD?

CLAY JONES
& JEAN E. JONES

HARVEST HOUSE PUBLISHERS
EUGENE, OREGON

All emphasis in Scripture quotations is added by the authors.

The information presented in this book is meant to be used for general resource purposes only. It is not intended to serve as a mental health or medical guide, nor should it substitute medical advice from a health care professional. If you have or think you may have a medical problem, speak to your doctor or health care practitioner immediately about your risk and possible treatments. Do not engage in any therapy or treatment without consulting a mental health or medical professional.

Cover design by Studio Gearbox

Cover image © IgorZh / Shutterstock

Interior design by KUHN Design Group

For bulk, special sales, or ministry purchases, please call 1-800-547-8979.
Email: CustomerService@hhpbooks.com

How Does God Use Suffering for Our Good?

Published by Harvest House Publishers
Eugene, Oregon 97408
www.harvesthousepublishers.com

ISBN 978-0-7369-9223-7 (pbk)
ISBN 978-0-7369-9224-4 (eBook)

Library of Congress Control Number: 2025936268

Printed in the United States of America

25 26 27 28 29 30 31 32 33 / BP / 10 9 8 7 6 5 4 3 2 1

"*How Does God Use Suffering for Our Good?* is a rare blend of biblical insight and real-world wisdom from two thoughtful authors who have firsthand experience with the topic. Clay and Jean Jones tackle one of life's toughest questions with the investigative rigor and clarity I value as a detective. Their seven practical truths offer not just answers, but genuine hope for anyone navigating hardship."

—**J. Warner Wallace,** Dateline-featured cold-case detective and author of *Cold-Case Christianity* and *The Truth in True Crime*

"Clay and Jean E. have provided such a gift to the church with this book. In transparently sharing their own journey of suffering, they model a theologically robust and God-glorifying faith that will bring readers both comfort and strength for the darkest times. Every one of us will endure dark times—the only question is how we'll respond. The powerful insights in this book offer answers that will bring you peace no matter the trial."

—**Natasha Crain,** speaker, podcaster, and author of five books, including *When Culture Hates You*

"Here is a profound and intensely practical book that looks unflinchingly at our struggles and provides a biblical pathway toward victory. My friends Clay and Jean E. Jones speak from personal experience about how we can find hope and meaning through the valleys of life. Take an eye-opening and heart-enlarging journey with them, and you'll emerge encouraged, uplifted, and—though it may seem counterintuitive—ever more grateful to God."

—**Lee Strobel,** bestselling author of *The Case for Christ* and *Seeing the Supernatural*

"There are a lot of books on God and suffering, but *How Does God Use Suffering for Our Good?* stands out for a few reasons. First, it is rooted in firsthand experience. Both Clay and Jean share personal hurt and suffering that frames the entire book. Second, it is biblical. Scripture is the authoritative source for all the wisdom and advice that flows from this book. Third, it is deeply honest. The Joneses do not shy away from difficult questions about suffering. They lean into them, and yet they offer wisdom to face them with hope and joy. I could not recommend this book more highly."

—**Sean McDowell, PhD,** is a professor of apologetics at Talbot School of Theology, the author or editor of more than 20 books, and a popular YouTuber

"When you're struggling, it's easy for people to whisper sweet lies full of cherry-picked scriptures with 'scriptural promises.' And that may make you feel good for a little while…until real life comes crashing down, demolishing all these simplistic notions of how life is supposed to be for a Christian. When that happens, you need real answers and real comfort. That is what this book provides. The Christian life is full of suffering—which is exactly what God promised us! There is no plan B for the Christian. In *How Does God Use Suffering for Our Good?*, Clay and Jean E. Jones provide biblical comfort with biblical encouragement (i.e., infusing courage!) in the face of life's toughest problems. And they don't lob these truth bombs from afar; they walk with them daily in their lives. I have seen it firsthand. If you as a Christian want to know how to honor God and have joy within suffering, then this is the book for you."

—**Hillary Morgan Ferrer,** founder/president of *Mama Bear Apologetics®*. Primary author/editor of *Mama Bear Apologetics®: Empowering Your Kids to Challenge Cultural Lies* and *Mama Bear Apologetics® Guide to Sexuality and Gender Identity: Empowering Your Kids to Understand and Live Out God's Design*

"What does a ministry-minded Christian couple do when they experience five miscarriages, numerous disappointments, doubts, unanswered prayer, and incurable cancer? They praise God and write a comforting and brilliant new book that will help thousands of others experiencing pain and suffering. Clay and Jean E. Jones reveal from their own lives and the Scriptures how God uses even the most devastating events for good both now and in eternity. This is as real as it gets, folks. Read and be encouraged!"

—**Frank Turek,** author and speaker

Thank You, Father, for how You use suffering to care for us.

ACKNOWLEDGMENTS

We wish to thank Harvest House Publishers for giving us the opportunity through this book to share our lived experience regarding the things that have been so helpful to us in our own endurance of suffering. In particular, we thank Nate Miller for his careful editing of and suggestions for our manuscript, and Steve Miller who helped initially guide and promote this project. Thank you also to the Harvest House cover design team for their excellent cover design direction. We thank God for the many people who have encouraged us in this project. But most of all, we thank God for His graciously using suffering in our lives to make us more like Him and to prepare us for a glorious eternity where we will enjoy Him and each other forever and ever.

CONTENTS

PREFACE

What if the Lord appeared to you in an unambiguous and unmistakable vision and said that in three years you would be moving to Belize where you would spend the rest of your life? Unless you had already frequented Belize, we suspect that the moment the vision ended you would Google "Belize." We also suspect that in the days that followed, you would continue to seek more information on Belize. Where might you live? What would you do? What might you eat? Crime rate? Climate? And so on. After all, if you knew with absolute certainty that you were going to live in Belize, you would want to prepare for that, right?

Although it's not impossible, it's unlikely that any of us are going to get an unambiguous and unmistakable vision telling us we're going to move to Belize, or anywhere else for that matter. We humans know nothing *absolutely, positively for sure* about our future other than the fact that one day, we, and everyone we know, will die. We don't know with absolute certainty what will happen tomorrow (after all, we could die in our sleep tonight—it happens). But there is one thing we do know for sure: Unless we die young and suddenly, we are all going to experience suffering and die.

Although some people suffer more than others—sometimes much, much more than others—unless one dies young and suddenly, we won't get out of this life without suffering. After all, as I (Clay) like to tell groups I am speaking to, "Only one thing will prevent you from watching everyone you know die from murder, accident, or disease and that will be your own death from murder, accident, or disease." When I say this, I usually add, "So have a nice day!" Then after a pause I kid, "But when I die, I want to die like my grandfather died—peacefully and in his sleep—not screaming like the passengers in his car."[1] The audience always laughs heartily because we're dealing with a hard truth. Unless one dies young and suddenly, no one is getting out of *this life* without immense suffering. The good news of the gospel is that in Jesus we can live forever! We'll talk a lot about that in the pages to come.

If the only thing we know absolutely, positively for sure about our future is that we are going to suffer and then die, we should prepare for that! Shouldn't we make sure we are ready? This makes sense, right? The two of us (Clay and Jean) have endured a lot of suffering in our lives and we have been striving to do what the Bible teaches in preparation for suffering—seeking to do what the Bible says when suffering strikes. The good news is we can tell you that we have been victorious over suffering, and you can be too. The best preparation is to have a robust view of the glory that will await us throughout eternity, for heaven will be gloriously better than whatever we could ask or think (Ephesians 3:20). We'll talk about that much more in what follows.

HOW WE CAME TO WRITE THIS BOOK

We started writing this book about two years prior to our finding out Clay had metastasized cancer. Although many Christians start writing books on suffering after they find out they are seriously ill, that's not why we started writing *How Does God Use Suffering for Our Good?* We have both been Word-abiding Christians for more than 50 years, and during that time have always seen our Lord turn suffering into our good. In fact, as you will see, how God has used suffering in our lives is not simply good, but great.

WHAT WE COVER

This book is about how to be victorious in suffering. All believers can be victorious and triumphant in suffering. The history of the Christian church abounds with examples of those who have been victorious in suffering—we will mention many of them. We intend to be very specific in how we have overcome our own suffering, so this book is not theoretical—we have lived and are living what we write in these pages.

This book is not a book about the larger question of why God allows evil. Clay already published a well-regarded book on that subject entitled *Why Does God Allow Evil?: Compelling Answers for Life's Toughest Questions* (Harvest House, 2017). In that book, Clay answers such questions as why we suffer for Adam's sin, why God allows children to suffer, the destiny of the unevangelized, the fairness of hell, the nature of free will, and how our glorious eternity will dwarf our suffering on earth to insignificance.

Regarding the seven truths that comprise most of this book, we really do practice them—regularly! What follows isn't theory. We really employ the truths we'll describe and, not shockingly, it turns out that doing what God says to do has immensely helped us.

A LITTLE ABOUT US

For years, Clay taught a graduate-level course, "Why God Allows Evil," in the Christian Apologetics program at Talbot School of Theology. Responding to student questions and objections honed his answers about evil and suffering. Clay then authored *Why Does God*

Allow Evil?: Compelling Answers for Life's Toughest Questions (Harvest House, 2017). Later he published a book on how the Christian can experience victory in facing death entitled *Immortal: How the Fear of Death Drives Us and What We Can Do About It* (Harvest House, 2020).

Jean has always been involved in all of Clay's teaching and writing. She edited all his books and articles, and she honed and originated many of the concepts he taught. In addition, Jean is the coauthor of five women's Bible studies. *Discovering Hope in the Psalms* (Harvest House, 2017) demonstrates how to pray psalms of lament when suffering. *Discovering Joy in Philippians* (Harvest House, 2019) explains how to build joy amid difficulties. *Discovering Jesus in the Old Testament* (Harvest House, 2019) and *Discovering Good News in John* (Harvest House, 2022) strengthen faith as they explore why and how Jesus suffered for us to bring us into the glorious kingdom of God. *Discovering Wisdom in Proverbs* (Harvest House, 2023) embraces Scripture's time-honored truths about how to live a blessed life.

INTRODUCTION

PREPARING TO CONQUER

C.S. Lewis writes, "Scripture and tradition habitually put the joys of heaven into the scale against the sufferings of earth, and no solution of the problem of pain that does not do so can be called a Christian one."[1] Sadly, however, an overwhelming majority of books on suffering barely give the "joys of heaven" a nod. I (Clay) recently reviewed a book sent to me on how to help those who are suffering based on the author's own suffering, but it saddened me because it had little to say about the glory that awaits us for eternity. Regrettably for many, the glory of eternity has become an also-ran doctrine. The glory we are to receive is underappreciated, and so eternity becomes the "P.S." to the Christian life.

Glory is an odd word.[2] It is the strongest word that communicates magnificence, courage, resplendence, beauty, worthiness, honor, and renown. Americans call their flag "Old Glory." We use glory to describe our army's victory in battle. Sometimes, we say that mountains and sunsets are glorious. At times people will attribute glory to themselves or something they've done (for example, computer gamers sometimes talk about their glorious victories). But humans rarely refer to other humans as glorious except sarcastically: "There he is in all his glory." *Glorious* means "possessing or deserving glory: illustrious," "marked by great beauty or splendor: magnificent," or "delightful, wonderful."[3]

We humans long for glory, and for Christians to be victorious over, to overcome, and to conquer suffering we absolutely, positively must revel in our glorious eternal future. In fact, Paul tells the Colossians that he always thanks God for them because "we have heard of your faith in Christ Jesus and of the love you have for all God's people—the faith and love that *spring* from the hope stored up for you in heaven" (Colossians 1:4-5 NIV).[4] Notice that faith and love "spring" from the hope of heaven. So important is hope that, as Richard R. Melick writes in his commentary on Colossians, it provides "the basis for Christian growth since the most basic elements of faith toward God and love toward others grow out of hope. In reality, without hope there is no reason for faith or love, and everything is directed to ourselves and our world."[5] Indeed. Consider that if in life we were simply going to watch everyone we love die and then die ourselves, and there was no future, no hope beyond that, then what good could spring from that despair? Even if we believed there was a God, it would be hard to live a life of love if we thought that, ultimately, we would cease to exist. Our hope is the desire and expectation of a great eternity where we will be welcomed into God's presence and reunited with loved ones. Without hope it would be impossible not to be self-interested and faithless. How could we have faith without the hope of a glorious eternity? As Hebrews 11:1 puts it, "Faith is the assurance of things hoped for, the conviction of things not seen." Faith and the hope of eternity are inextricably linked. You can't have one without the other. The brighter our view of eternal glory, the more easily we will overcome the sufferings of this life.

REALISTIC EXPECTATIONS ABOUT VICTORY OVER SUFFERING

Now, we must be clear. We're not saying that we, or anyone else, are ever going to write anything that will make suffering only tickle. We're not saying that being victorious in suffering will mean that believers won't mourn, cry—even sob—or be in pain. We don't mean that we've never had teary, sad days—we've had many! Jesus wept (Luke 19:41; John 11:35), and Jesus says, "Blessed are those who mourn" (Matthew 5:4). But Christians can be victorious while suffering (even when crying our eyes out). By this we mean two things.

The first way believers can have a victorious day while suffering is by honoring God through suffering, even if experiencing immense emotional or physical pain. We have done this habitually. We have honored God and thanked Him for the hardship we were enduring in the moment we were enduring it. For example, in January 2004, Clay was in immense pain and was diagnosed with an incurable cancer. After we hung up the phone with the oncologist, with tears streaming down our faces, we immediately prayed a prayer of thanksgiving to God. At that moment, we knew we had honored God in suffering and had defeated Satan in the heavenly places. We have prayed similar prayers amid other sufferings, and we have been victorious in the heavenly realms because of it. We will say more about this later.

The second way Christians can have victory while suffering is by rejoicing in the glory that God is working in us precisely because we are suffering. Paul wrote, "We rejoice in hope of the glory of God. Not only that, but we rejoice in our sufferings" (Romans 5:2-3). James wrote, "Count it all joy, my brothers, when you meet trials of various kinds, for you know that the testing of your faith produces steadfastness. And let steadfastness have its full effect, that you may be *perfect and complete, lacking in nothing*" (James 1:2-4). Peter wrote, "You have been grieved by various trials, so that the tested genuineness of your faith...may be found to result in praise and glory and honor at the revelation of Jesus Christ" (1 Peter 1:6-7). In other words, we can have a sense of joy while suffering. The parents of brides or grooms do this all the time. They're sad to "lose" a son or daughter but thankful for the blessing their child is about to receive. Likewise, women in labor are often in immense pain but can also rejoice that soon their suffering will be rewarded by the birth of a child. Similarly, recognizing that our suffering—our "light momentary affliction," as Paul calls it—"is preparing for us an eternal weight of glory beyond all comparison" (2 Corinthians 4:17) enables us to rejoice in a glory that transcends any earthly hardship. We can be victorious in suffering by realizing that suffering prepares us for eternal glory.

IS THIS WORKS RIGHTEOUSNESS?

At the outset, we must answer a question that might confuse some Christians. Repeatedly, we will quote verses like 2 Timothy 2:12, "If we *endure* we will also reign with him"; Revelation 21:7 (NIV), "Those who are *victorious* will inherit all this, and I will be their God and they will be my children"; Revelation 3:21 (NIV), "To the one who is *victorious*, I will give the right to sit with me on my throne, just as I was victorious and sat down with my Father on his throne"; and so on. These verses are *not* teaching works righteousness. We are not saved by our own goodness. We have not forgotten about the Protestant Reformation. We are indeed saved by grace alone through faith alone. But there is a reformation maxim from John Calvin that applies: "Faith alone saves but the faith that saves is never alone."[6] Here are the first three theses of Martin Luther's *95 Theses* that began the Reformation in earnest:

1. When our Lord and Master Jesus Christ said, "Repent" (Mt 4:17), he willed the entire life of believers to be one of repentance.

2. This word cannot be understood as referring to the sacrament of penance, that is, confession and satisfaction, as administered by the clergy.

3. Yet it does not mean solely inner repentance; such inner

> repentance is worthless unless it produces various outward mortification of the flesh.[7]

Notice that Luther said that a person is not repenting at all unless that repentance changes the person's behavior.[8] This makes sense because people live their lives based on what they sincerely believe, and if you sincerely believe that Jesus really is God who died for our sins and was raised from the dead, that He is coming back to judge the world, and that all of eternity awaits, you will live in accord with those beliefs.

WHAT TO DO NOW: PRAY FOR REVELATION ABOUT THE GLORY THAT AWAITS

Therefore, dear Christian, we urge you to stop and pray right now that God will give you a revelation of the glory that awaits us in heaven forever. That revelation will enable you to be victorious over suffering.

PREPARING TO SUFFER

About 20 years ago, I (Clay) was speaking on why God allows evil to around 40 to 50 guys crammed into a Biola University men's dorm. When finished, I took questions. The last question that night was, "Do you have any general advice for us?" I was surprised and asked what kind of advice the young man was looking for. He replied, "I don't know, just any general advice?" I responded, "Well, yes, I do: *READ the Bible and DO what it says!*" He said, "That's simple." And it is simple—not easy, but simple. But, sadly, so few Christians actually do this. Yet this is what every Bible-believing pastor I know considers "basic Christianity." Christians not only need to read the Bible; they need to abide in the Bible and do what it says. Abiding in God's

Word is the first action that prepares us for the disasters, panics, and inevitable suffering that life always brings.

In Luke 6:46-48, Jesus says,

> Why do you call me "Lord, Lord," and not do what I tell you? Everyone who comes to me and hears my words and does them, I will show you what he is like: he is like a man building a house, who dug deep and laid the foundation on the rock. And when a flood arose, the stream broke against that house and could not shake it, because it had been well built.

But then, in verse 49, Jesus warns that the one who only hears His words but does not do them "is like a man who built a house on the ground without a foundation. When the stream broke against it, immediately it fell, and the ruin of that house was great." The bottom line: Jesus says that only those who hear God's Word *and do it* will survive calamity.

Even non-Christians like the saying, "You will know the truth, and the truth will set you free." But few know that Jesus gave a condition: "If you abide in my word, you are truly my disciples, and you will know the truth, and the truth will set you free" (John 8:31-32). You truly are *not* Jesus' disciple unless you abide in Jesus' Word; and that doesn't mean you simply read a verse now and then. Similarly, in Psalm 1:2-3, we read about the one whose "delight is in the law of the Lord, and on his law he meditates day and night. He is like a tree planted by streams of water that yields its fruit in its season, and its leaf does not wither. In all that he does, he prospers." If we immerse ourselves in the Word of God, then when suffering strikes, we can wield "the sword of the Spirit" (Ephesians 6:17). If we're immersed in the Word of God, when trouble comes, we won't need to ask, "What would Jesus do?" because we will already know what Jesus would do.

Second, Christians need to be in prayer. As you will read in these pages, there have been many times in prayer while suffering that a Bible verse or idea has been quickened to us. While in prayer, we've seen passages that we have read for years in a new light. And of course, the Lord has granted many of our requests. James 4:2 says, "You do not have, because you do not ask."[9] That means that we need to do His will. If we don't do His will, we will be like any child—we won't want to approach our Father because our heart knows He has some things He wants to say that we won't want to hear. So keep a clear conscience and pray.

Jesus says in Matthew 6:6, "When you pray, go into your room and shut the door and pray to your Father who is in secret. And your Father who sees in secret will reward you." To that I (Clay) say, "CASH IN!" Occasionally, when I've said that, some Christians have accused me of sounding too mercenary or reward oriented. But why not? Jesus told us that if we pray privately, our Father will reward us, and I want the rewards God offers, don't you? If the richest man in the world told you he'd reward you if you prayed or fasted without telling anyone, I'll bet the overwhelming majority of readers would give it a shot. Well, the Creator of the universe says, "Pray or fast, and I will reward you." Cash in!

Third, Christians need to be in fellowship. It's not enough to simply attend a Sunday service. We need to be in small groups or at least make sure we regularly see true Christian friends. When hardship occurs, we need to be able to rely on each other. After all, we can't do any of the following unless we're actually in regular fellowship with each other.

- "Love one another" and "outdo one another in showing honor" (Romans 12:10)—the suffering need love and honor.
- "Instruct one another" (Romans 15:14)—the suffering often need to be reminded of scriptural truth.

- "Serve one another" (Galatians 5:13)—does someone need something repaired, or a ride?
- "Encourag[e] one another" (Hebrews 10:25)—who doesn't need encouragement?
- "Pray for one another" (James 5:16)—that is helpful and may bring healing!
- "Show hospitality to one another" (1 Peter 4:9)—when Clay first had cancer, we loved it when people brought us meals.

We've known Christians who've withdrawn from fellowship when suffering struck. Three years ago, when I (Clay) found out I had metastasized cancer, I immediately called for the elders of my church to pray for me and anoint me with oil (James 5:14), and they were glad to do it. Frankly, the day they prayed I thought it possible that I might only live another six months, but here I am at the time of this writing without any symptoms caused by the cancer. I post about our odyssey on Facebook, and I'm thankful for the many people who respond and tell me they are praying for us. Further, I have a rather large mailing list of Christian friends, many of whom aren't on Facebook, and I email them with regular updates and prayer requests. We love the support we receive from these posts and emails.

Many have shared how our openness about my struggles with cancer has encouraged their faith. Here is an example from social media: "It must seem surprising to a lot of folks that you both have so much confidence in God's love and goodness during what is for most folks a terrifying and depressing situation. But your abiding trust makes perfect sense to some of us."

Fourth, we've found that in times of suffering, keeping what we call a truth journal helps immensely. Our truth journals contain truths, Scriptures, and remembrances of God's good care. Clay's truth journal is a simple Word document with headings like "Truths to Remember,"

"Encouraging Scriptures," and "Remembering How God Has Worked Out Good for Us." Jean's is more elaborate and is handwritten in a notebook. She has pages headed "Truths," "Remembrances," "Scripture," "Prayers," "Prayer Requests and Answers," and "Good." We both list the seven truths we'll be discussing in the following pages as well as other truths we find helpful during hard times. We'll talk more about how we use our journals in upcoming chapters.

One thing of which to be aware: If you are a true Christian but are not abiding in God's Word, not praying, or not in fellowship, our Lord will often use suffering to drive you toward obeying His commands.

WHERE'S GOD?

C.S. Lewis in *The Screwtape Letters* answered well the question of why we don't have more evidence for God's existence, especially while suffering. Screwtape is a senior tempter who writes to Wormwood, a junior tempter, about how to tempt Christians. He refers to God as the "Enemy." Screwtape writes to Wormwood: "You must have often wondered why the Enemy does not make more use of His power to be sensibly present to human souls in any degree He chooses and at any moment. But you now see that the Irresistible and the Indisputable are the two weapons which the very nature of His scheme forbids Him to use."[10] Indeed, as Clay has written elsewhere, God gives enough evidence of His existence so that those who want to believe will have their beliefs justified but not so much that those who don't want to believe will be forced to feign loyalty.[11] Lewis continues: "Merely to override a human will (as His felt presence in any but the faintest and more mitigated degree would certainly do) would be for Him useless. He cannot ravish, He can only woo. For His ignoble idea is to eat the cake and have it; the creatures are to be one with Him, but yet themselves; merely to cancel them, or assimilate them, will not serve."[12] And that's where suffering comes in. The Lord doesn't make His presence, His existence, too obvious. As Screwtape points out, and as we will be discussing shortly, it is during suffering that we grow into the kind of creature He wants us to be. Screwtape was correct to write: "Do not be deceived, Wormwood. Our cause is never more in danger than when a human, no longer desiring, but still intending, to do our Enemy's will, looks round upon a universe from which every trace of Him seems to have vanished, and asks why he has been forsaken, and still obeys."[13] Exactly. When we honor God through suffering, we threaten the devil and his angels. We will rightfully participate in their judgment.

WHAT TO DO NOW: PRAY FOR REVELATION OF THE GREATNESS OF YOUR SALVATION

At the outset, we want to encourage you to pray that God gives you a revelation of the greatness of your salvation. Paul prayed for all the saints that God would do that in Ephesians 1:17-19:

> I keep asking that the God of our Lord Jesus Christ, the glorious Father, may give you the Spirit of wisdom and revelation, so that you may know him better. I pray that the eyes of your heart may be enlightened in order that you may know the hope to which he has called you, the riches of his glorious inheritance in his holy people, and his incomparably great power for us who believe (NIV).

We encourage you to pray this prayer and study the things for which Paul asks. A robust view of eternal life in Jesus will immensely help you face the hardships of this life victoriously and will help free you from worldly lusts.[14]

THE BLESSINGS THE LORD HAS FOR OUR ETERNITY

If we continue to honor God through suffering, then we are victorious conquerors who will be glorified throughout eternity. Thus, shortly we will look at the blessings that the Lord has for our eternity, especially as laid out in the book of Revelation.[15] These are the blessings that the Lord promises to those who are victorious, who overcome, and who conquer.

But conquer, overcome, and be victorious over what? We need to conquer, overcome, and be victorious over suffering in its various forms: sickness, accidents, temptations to compromise, and persecution, even when these things might result in our deaths. But if we do conquer, if we do overcome, if we are victorious by honoring God despite whatever this fallen world throws at us, then we'll receive eternal blessings.

All these blessings climax with the promise of inheriting eternal life. And, of course, that resolves our deepest need. We need to know that we will not cease to exist at the death of our bodies, but that we are going to be welcomed into a wonderful life everlasting where there will be no more death or mourning or crying or pain.

Please note a couple of things about the phrase, "He who has an ear, let him hear what the Spirit says to the churches" (Revelation 2:7; see also 2:11; 2:17; 2:29; 3:6; 3:13; 3:22). This is a divine "Listen up!" said "to the one who conquers." All these messages culminate in a great heavenly blessing. True followers of Jesus will resonate with those blessings or warnings, but the spiritually apathetic will hear only, "He who has an ear, let him hear, blah, blah, blah." The unspiritual person will hear this as only some sort of religiously fantastical falderal. Even though true followers of Jesus may not understand all the Lord is saying in His Word—especially in the book of Revelation—they will still recognize that these blessings are significant and that something out of this world awaits them.

Let us remember that it is the Lord who created all the pleasures; Satan never created even one of them. As David wrote in Psalm 16:11, "You make known to me the path of life; in your presence there is fullness of joy; at your right hand are pleasures forevermore." Here on earth, it is the Lord who gives us pleasures like great food, wine, and sex. It is the Lord who makes orgasms possible. You may think we used the word *orgasms* to shock you. And indeed, we did! To shock you out of the satanically inspired stupor that heaven is a place you don't want to be.[16] The Lord gives us those pleasures on earth, and if in heaven there isn't sex as we now know it, then we should expect better things in its place. In fact, Christians sometimes ask if this or that favorite thing of theirs will be in heaven—cats, mountains, trains (a friend of ours really likes trains)—and the answer, again, is that if some of the things we really enjoy aren't there, then we should expect better things in their place.

In response to Clay's blog saying these things, a woman sent him a Facebook direct message:

> What an impactful and convicting blog post! I have definitely fallen victim to the idea that perfection equals an absence of pleasure. I have also slid into the belief that heaven is a place of sterile holiness—I almost imagine a Catholic convent or something—in which I would struggle to fit. Your post really spoke to my heart and soul and has challenged me to get back into God's word about heaven. I have allowed my human fear of death to negatively color this topic for too long. Seriously, I am so thankful…

She's not alone. It's the rare Christian who doesn't have a dour view of eternity, and we seek in this book to help change that.

1

TRUTHS ABOUT VICTORY IN SUFFERING

My gynecologist's certainty gave me confidence. In a booming voice, incongruously deep for his small stature, he assured me that my baby was well, and I needn't be worried over an earlier miscarriage. So Clay and I joyfully celebrated the three-month milestone marking the pregnancy as safe.[1]

It seemed life was unfolding just as we'd hoped: We'd married, Clay had completed seminary, and soon after his graduation, he was offered an associate pastorate at a large church. With a baby on the way, we once again had reason to celebrate.

A week after that prenatal visit, we headed to a beach-front hotel for a church staff conference. After a laughter-filled dinner full of excited chatter and congratulations over expecting our first child, I excused myself and sleepily returned to the hotel room. There, sitting in a stark white bathroom, I stared in shock at a bright red streak.

No, no—this couldn't be happening.

The unfamiliar room, with its too perfectly arranged furniture and jarringly cheerful seascapes, amplified my disbelief. Mechanically, I crawled into the strange bed. I tugged at the cold sheet and foreign blanket, desperate for any bit of comfort, then pulled my Bible near.

"God, You know I've begged You to protect this baby," I prayed. "God, please! I can't cope with another miscarriage. Please heal my body and stop the bleeding. Please, don't let me lose my baby."

A couple hours later, Clay came in. He saw the anxiety in my expression and wrapped me in warm arms.

In the morning, we quietly drove home. By evening, labor began, and I fought with everything in me to stop it. But by daylight, the battle was lost.

Difficult years followed, as my dream of motherhood shifted from joyous hope to desperate pleading, to the grief of impossibility—and finally, to settled acceptance that it wasn't to be. Looking back, I can see that contentment with childlessness was a journey with four major milestones. It began with changing what I mistakenly believed was a faith-filled response to difficulties.

FOUR MAJOR MILESTONES

Milestone 1: Developing an "Open-Eyed" Faith

Like many Christians, I'd memorized verses such as "All things work together for good" (Romans 8:28) and "Give thanks in all circumstances" (1 Thessalonians 5:18). When bad things happened, I'd quote these verses, express my gratitude that God would eventually make everything right, and push away my questions. Trying to trust God, I did something akin to closing my eyes, putting my hands over my ears, and saying, "La-la-la-la—just have faith—la-la-la-la."

Giving thanks through the first miscarriage wasn't as difficult because the pregnancy was unplanned. Clay was still in school, and I had a new job; I concluded it wasn't the time for us to have children. The second miscarriage was different: We were ready to start a family, and I couldn't identify any "good" that might result from our loss. Nonetheless, I quoted verses, thanked God, and made every effort to stay positive. "It must be God's will, so it's fine with me," I told my friends.

I thought I was doing well spiritually. At least, I didn't feel angry with God. Actually, I didn't feel anything toward God. That vaguely concerned me, but I wrote it off as emotional exhaustion.

Then one afternoon, I discovered that a houseguest had stacked my get-well cards out of sight. Furious, I wanted to scream, "How dare you move my things without asking me?" I grabbed the cards, slapped them on the coffee table, and sank into the sofa.

What's wrong with me? I wondered. Slowly I realized I might be angry. And worse, I might be angry with God. *Is that even safe?*

I picked up my Bible and scanned the concordance for "anger." Passages described God as slow to anger and full of understanding and compassion. *Perhaps it's okay to tell God what I'm feeling.*

I went for a walk to be alone with God and came upon an empty schoolyard.

"God, I think I might be angry," I prayed, stuffing my hands into my jeans pockets. "It's possible that I might even be mad at You."

A dried-out patch of dirt caught my eye. Its barrenness irked me: There should have been grass in that spot, not scraggly weeds. I kicked at a rock that was partly buried in the dirt.

"God, I *am* angry. How could You allow another miscarriage when I repeatedly told You that I couldn't handle it?"

Emotion-charged words began to flow freely. I pressed God with every question: "I'm Your child—why did You let this happen to me?" I exposed every fear: "I won't be able to enjoy a future pregnancy! And how can I face those church members who think my miscarriage was due to a lack of faith?" I expressed every hurt, particularly that I felt inadequate as a woman. And I listed every reason why I thought God should have intervened.

"Everyone else can have children—why can't I?"

As soon as those words came out of my mouth, I knew I'd misspoken.

Many women cannot have children; some also have no husband. Then it hit me: I'd felt entitled to motherhood. This was the root of my anger. I felt God had denied me a "right."

I stepped into the street to avoid a row of oleanders, glancing at the glossy evergreens filled with clusters of red, pink, and white flowers. They bloomed almost year-round despite scorching temperatures, drought, and poor soil—the same soil that only a few steps back barely supported a scattering of weeds. *Is this what You want from me, God: to grow and blossom despite tough circumstances?*

Hesitantly, I began to thank God for His love and faithfulness—only a truly loving Father would allow His child to come beat on His chest. It was difficult at first, but I recognized that in His infinite wisdom, God had allowed a circumstance that would cause me to grow. While I still couldn't identify any specific good that would result from my loss, now I could acknowledge, by faith, that God would indeed work it out.

This change in me was subtle, but significant. In the past, whenever trials occurred, I closed my eyes to the problem, thinking it was good to shut out anything that might challenge my faith. But while closed eyes can't see problems, they also can't see God.

When I "opened my eyes"—presenting my problems and questions to God rather than hiding from them—I began to find answers and understand God better. As a result, my faith in God's goodness grew.

Milestone 2: Choosing God's Will

After the second miscarriage, my doctor boomed assurances that there was still nothing to worry about. I asked if there was a point at which having a child became less likely. He answered with too much finality, "After five sequential miscarriages, it's impossible."

A third loss soon followed. Avoiding my eyes, he ordered numerous tests. Weeks later, I sat eagerly at his desk, awaiting answers that would fix everything. Still evading eye contact, he said nothing had been found except a low hormone that couldn't be replaced without causing birth defects. I'm not sure how I managed to reach the car before bursting into tears.

Reluctantly, I began to face that Clay and I might not have children. I felt I'd always meant it when I told God, "Thy will be done." And while I wanted to submit fully to God's will, I couldn't quite let go of my desire to be a mom.

One day, while asking God to help me surrender my will, I remembered another prayer from years before. As a young Christian, on realizing the totality of God's forgiveness, I'd prayed with immense gratitude, "God, if You never answer another prayer for me, that's fine. Salvation is enough."

Now I felt God whispering, "Did you mean it?"

Instantly, I was ready to answer. The miscarriages—even childlessness—were miniscule compared to the enormous and costly gift of salvation. Resolutely, I told God, "Yes, I meant it. Salvation is enough." When I chose God's will over my own, I took a big step toward contentment.

Milestone 3: Seeking an Eternal Perspective

Clay and I discussed adoption, but the cost was out of reach on a pastor's budget. Besides, what if God had a special ministry in mind for us? We ruled adoption out.

I wondered if my life could be fulfilling without children. As I searched the Bible and prayed, I realized that having children was not eternally valuable in itself, while having one's faith refined is of great value to all believers (1 Peter 1:6-8). God so valued my faith that He used the losses to expose and remove impurities, such as false beliefs and fear-based responses. Plus, by faithfully enduring hardships, I'd gain something forever valuable: an eternal glory that would far outweigh earthly losses (2 Corinthians 4:17). The more I grasped this eternal perspective, the more content I became.

Milestone 4: Offering Sacrificial Praise

At the fifth miscarriage, I mourned not only the loss of the baby, but the loss of ever bearing children. The lessons I'd learned were helping me to cope, but one question still stymied me. So I prayed, "God, Psalm 37:4 says if I delight myself in You, You'll give me the desires of my heart. I *am* delighting myself in You. I don't understand. Why aren't You giving me the desire of my heart?" Once again, I sensed a question to me: "What is the greatest desire of your heart?" My answer came with ease, "Following You, God."

At that moment, I realized all of life involves choosing between conflicting desires. Our choices reveal what we value most. I suddenly understood sacrificial praise (Hebrews 13:15) in a new way: choosing to praise and glorify God by relinquishing something costly. I wanted to offer sacrificial praise, but finding the words was hard, so I pictured my prayer.

I imagined placing my desire for children and the question "Why?" in a box. I wrapped the box with pale green paper and tied it with gold ribbon, then placed it at the foot of Jesus' cross, which shone softly through a dark night at the bottom of a hill.

I prayed, "This is my gift to You. On Resurrection Day, if You want to open this gift and show me 'Why?'—that's fine. And if You don't, that's fine too—I think answers won't be a priority when I'm overjoyed by being with You."

As the days went on, every time I hurt, every time I yearned, I brought this same picture to mind and prayed, "This is my gift to You." That picture and prayer brought me peace.

A QUESTION ABOUT SUFFERING TO WHICH EVERYONE WANTS AN ANSWER

We started this chapter with Jean's story because it illustrates how younger Christians may grow through major suffering. We must learn the subtle difference between a faith that relies on closing our eyes to problems and a faith that sees problems clearly while still trusting God.

For now, let us begin with the most common question about suffering: *Why does God allow so much suffering?*

Angels, cherubim, seraphim, the living creatures, and other heavenly beings must be appalled when they see us people on planet Earth: the depravities, diseases, disabilities, depressions, and deaths rampant among the inhabitants of our planet. These horrors were at one time completely foreign to them. Prior to Satan's rebellion, every creature was whole, was healthy, and had enough of everything; plus, no one ever died! But now the heavenly beings, like us here on earth, see the damage that sin has wrought.

Thankfully, though, *this life* isn't all there is. By *this life* we mean this earthly life, which—if you are a true believer in Jesus as Lord—is only the beginning of eternal life. In the kingdom to come, as it says in Revelation 21:4, "He will wipe away every tear from their eyes, and death shall be no more, neither shall there be mourning, nor crying, nor pain anymore, for the former things have passed away."

As we mentioned in the preface, only one thing will prevent you from watching everyone you know die from murder, accident, or disease, and that will be your own death from murder, accident, or disease. So unless one dies young and suddenly, everyone is going to endure significant suffering. Indeed, some people are suffering much more than we think. We might think there are many people who aren't suffering much, but we often need to look deeper. Christina Onassis, heir to her father's shipping fortune, once said, "Happiness does not depend on money. Our family is the best proof of that." She continued, "Since the death of my mother and my brother, we have learned how short life can be and with what terrible suddenness death strikes."[2]

Clay often tells audiences that "God's plan A for your life is to take you through regular periods of suffering, and there is no plan

B." That's so true! In Philippians 1:29, Paul writes, "For it has been *granted to you* that for the sake of Christ you should not only believe in him but also suffer for his sake." Did you notice? Suffering has been "granted to you"! God is doing you a favor by allowing you to suffer for His sake. In John 16:33, Jesus says, "In the world you will have tribulation. But take heart; I have overcome the world." In Acts 14:19, 22, we read that a mob stoned Paul and dragged him out of the city, "supposing that he was dead." But Paul soon rose up and then was "strengthening the souls of the disciples, encouraging them to continue in the faith, and saying that through many tribulations we must enter the kingdom of God."

Of course, as we age, we all begin to suffer various diseases. But Paul says that's a good thing. Suffering is not incidental to being a Christian—it is integral, it is the plan, it has been "granted" to us, and the Lord expects us to respond to suffering in a God-honoring way in preparation for eternal glory. We're sad for the countless Christians who think Christianity is about our having little to no suffering in life on planet Earth. But an easy life isn't God's plan for the Christian, and it has never been the plan.

Now, here's good news. We've known Christians who were not spiritually reflective until suffering struck them or their loved ones, and then they poured the Bible into themselves. Suddenly, they read the Bible as if their lives depended on it (which they did—Matthew 4:4).

Our Lord does us a favor by allowing suffering to come into our lives. Just as human glory almost always comes through the suffering of hard work, eternal glory likewise comes through suffering. In fact, as was mentioned in the introduction, the word *glory* in the New Testament is regularly related to suffering (Luke 24:26; Romans 2:6-7; 5:2; 8:18; 2 Corinthians 4:17; Ephesians 3:13; 2 Timothy 2:10; Hebrews 2:10; 1 Peter 1:6-7; 5:1, 10).

In Romans 8:16-18, we encounter key verses about suffering. Paul writes,

> The Spirit himself bears witness with our spirit that we are children of God, and if children, then heirs—heirs of God and fellow heirs with Christ, *provided* we suffer with him in order that we may also be glorified with him. For I consider that the sufferings of this present time are not worth comparing with the glory that is to be revealed to us.

Paul is clear: We must "suffer with him" if we are going to inherit the kingdom and be glorified with Him.

THE IRONIC NATURE OF VICTORY IN SUFFERING

How do we live victoriously while suffering? G.K. Beale, in his commentary on Revelation, writes, " 'Overcomers' are those whose lives are characterized by refusal to compromise their faith despite the threat of persecution. They ironically conquer when they maintain their faith even though they may appear defeated in the world's eyes."[3] Revelation 5:1-3 gives us an example of this kind of ironic victory: "Then I saw in the right hand of him who sat on the throne a scroll with writing on both sides and sealed with seven seals. And I saw a mighty angel proclaiming in a loud voice, 'Who is worthy to break the seals and open the scroll?' But no one in heaven or on earth or under the earth could open the scroll or even look inside it" (NIV).

Then, in verse 4, John tells us of his agony, "I wept and wept because no one was found who was worthy to open the scroll or look inside" (NIV).[4] But in verse 5, we read, "And one of the elders said to me, 'Weep no more; behold, the Lion of the tribe of Judah, the Root of David, has conquered, so that he can open the scroll and its seven seals.' " What a relief! Jesus conquered and so is worthy to open the scroll.

But what John sees surprises him: "Then I saw a Lamb, as slain, standing at the center of the throne, encircled by the four living creatures and the elders."[5] The conqueror John sees a "slaughtered" Lamb![6] Not one lying dead but standing, very much alive. Beale explains,

> The present victorious effect of the Lamb's overcoming resides not only in the fact that the Lamb continues to "stand" but also in the fact that it continues to exist as a *slaughtered* Lamb…In addition to the resurrection, the defeat of death was itself ironically a victory for Christ. That is, Christ as a Lion overcame by being slaughtered as a Lamb.[7]

This is further illustrated by the fact that in His post-resurrection, glorified body, Jesus still bore His crucifixion wounds (John 20:25-27). Jesus isn't ashamed of His crucifixion wounds for they memorialize what is certainly the greatest act of heroism in cosmic history. Even though Jesus was physically defeated, He is spiritually victorious.

There's an amazing scriptural parallel to this passage in Revelation found in Romans 8. In Romans 8:35, Paul asks, "Who shall separate us from the love of Christ? Shall tribulation, or distress, or persecution, or famine, or nakedness, or danger, or sword?" In Revelation 5, Jesus the conqueror appears as a slaughtered Lamb. In Romans 8:36-37, Paul talks similarly about us Christians: "As it is written, 'For your sake we are being killed all the day long; we are regarded as sheep to be slaughtered.' No, *in* all these things we are more than conquerors through him who loved us." Notice again, that we are more than conquerors *in* all these sufferings, *not by going around them.* "More than conquerors" comes from the Greek words *huper* and *nike.* We get the English word "hyper" from *huper. Nike* (where Nike athletic wear gets its name) is translated in the New Testament usually as "be victorious," "overcome," or "conquer,"[8] and we will use those words interchangeably. The New American Standard Bible translates *hupernike* as "overwhelmingly conquer." As we honor God through suffering, whatever we face as Christians, we overwhelmingly conquer!

During World War II, Corrie ten Boom's family hid Jews at their home in the Netherlands. Ultimately, Nazis discovered her family's actions and sent her and her sister, Betsie, to prison camps. Their final camp was Ravensbrück. In her book *The Hiding Place*, Corrie writes about their time there. Betsie, who later died in Ravensbrück, read Romans 8—about our being more than conquerors—to Corrie and some of the other prisoners:

> I would look about us as Betsie read, watching the light leap from face to face. More than conquerors...It was not a wish. It was a fact. We knew it, we experienced it minute by minute—poor, hated, hungry. We are more than conquerors. Not "we shall be." We are! Life in Ravensbrück took place on two separate levels, mutually impossible. One, the observable, external life, grew every day more horrible. The other, the life we lived with God, grew daily better, truth upon truth, glory upon glory.[9]

And what do we overwhelmingly conquer? In Romans 8:35, Paul lists "tribulation, or distress, or persecution, or famine, or nakedness, or danger, or sword." *Tribulation* means "suffering or trouble, usually resulting from oppression"[10] and *distress* means "pain or suffering affecting the body, a bodily part, or the mind."[11] These words taken together apply to any suffering or hardship that comes upon a Christian—disability, dementia, accident, COVID, cancer, abuse, betrayed relationships, and so on. *Persecution* refers to mistreatment and hostility. *Famine* literally means "an extreme scarcity of food." *Nakedness* can mean "the state of being unclothed or stripped by force." Many Christians have been stripped naked and raped or otherwise sexually molested. The sexual molestation of Christians has happened many times from the time of the Roman Empire up to the current day. It's important to consider a hard truth: The Bible doesn't promise that we won't be stripped naked, raped, and tortured to death. Not only has that happened throughout the centuries, torture, rape, and murder of Christians still happens today. For example, while working for United Christian Ministries, 24-year-old Kayla Mueller was abducted by ISIS in Syria. Her captors pulled out her fingernails and made her a sex slave until they killed her two years later.[12] She remained faithful to Jesus. We must note, dear Christian, if you've been abused or sexually assaulted, whether as a child or an adult, nothing can happen to you in this life that will in any way diminish your eternity.

When it comes to tribulations and distresses, Paul writes in 2 Corinthians 11:23-25 that he was often imprisoned, experienced countless beatings, and was "often near death." He says, "Five times I received at the hands of the Jews the forty lashes less one. Three times I was beaten with rods. Once I was stoned. Three times I was shipwrecked; a night and a day I was adrift at sea." And then when it comes to danger, he writes in verses 26-27 that he was "in danger from rivers, danger from robbers, danger from my own people, danger from Gentiles, danger in the city, danger in the wilderness, danger at sea, danger from false brothers; in toil and hardship, through many a sleepless night, in hunger and thirst, often without food, in cold and exposure." When it comes to the sword, it is very likely that Paul was beheaded by Nero.[13]

Jesus honored God through suffering. In John 18:11, when soldiers came to arrest Jesus and Peter impulsively cut off the ear of one of the men, Jesus told Peter, "Put your sword away! Shall I not drink the cup the Father has given me?" (NIV). In other words, Jesus regarded all the horrific things that would soon happen to Him as part of the cup the Father had given Him, and He was going to do His Father's will regardless of how difficult it was. As D.A. Carson puts it, Jesus had a "firm resolution to accept what the Father gives him."[14] By doing His Father's will, Jesus was victorious. Jesus conquered. Similarly, we need to drink from the cup the Father has given us, and as we continue to honor our heavenly Father through whatever suffering He allows in our lives, then we are victorious, we overcome, and we conquer. As mentioned earlier, Paul writes in Romans 2:6-7, "He will render to each one according to his works: to those who by patience in well-doing seek for glory and honor and immortality, he will give eternal life." So let us seek glory, honor, and immortality!

A Roman triumph was a parade through the streets of Rome held in honor of the return of a victorious general. Harvard historian Mary Beard notes, "To be awarded a triumph was the most outstanding honor a Roman general could hope for."[15] In the parade, the general "would be drawn in a chariot—accompanied by the booty he had won, the prisoners he had taken captive, and his no doubt rowdy and raucous troops in their battle gear—through the streets of the city to the Temple of Jupiter on the Capitoline hill, where he would offer a sacrifice to the god."[16] It was the most lavish of all Roman rituals and was "celebrated more than three hundred times in the thousand-or-so-year history of the ancient city of Rome."[17] Triumphal arches celebrating the conquests of various generals remain in Rome, Algeria, Libya, Greece, and elsewhere.

In 2 Corinthians 2:14-16, Paul likens us to being slaves on parade in a Roman triumph: "But thanks be to God, who in Christ always leads us in triumphal procession, and through us spreads the fragrance of the knowledge of him everywhere. For we are the aroma of Christ to God among those who are being saved and among those who are perishing, to one a fragrance from death to death, to the other a fragrance from life to life." The world may smell defeat, but those of us in Christ are the fragrance of life.

Thus, Paul writes in 2 Corinthians 12:10, "I delight in weaknesses, in insults, in hardships, in persecutions, in difficulties. For when I am weak, then I am strong" (NIV). Are we getting this, dear Christian?

Hardship and persecution and difficulties are not our enemy. Worldliness is our enemy. A life of leisure is our enemy.[18] God uses hardships to make us the kind of person He insists that we become. David Garland explains that Paul's

> conquest by God actually allows him to take part in God's triumphant march as one now reconciled to God. Paul's theology is remarkable for its sense of paradox. He suffers with Christ in order to be glorified with him (Rom 8:17, 37). Victory comes in defeat; glory, in humiliation; and joy, in suffering (Col 1:24). The wise must become fools to become truly wise (1 Cor 3:18); the rich one becomes poor so that the poor might become rich (2 Cor 8:9).[19]

So as you and I follow Jesus' example and honor God in suffering, we conquer, we overcome, and we are victorious. When we honor God through suffering, we become like the apostles whose lives were always threatened. We "become a spectacle to the world, to angels, and to men" (1 Corinthians 4:9). We're not talking about Stoicism here, where you're supposed to act like everything is okay even when you're really hurting. Christianity isn't about "keeping a stiff upper lip." We Christians can cry our eyes out and still honor God in suffering—we (Clay and Jean) have done that many times!

Earlier we mentioned that ISIS abducted Kayla Mueller in Syria and made her into a sex slave.[20] Nonetheless, here's an excerpt from a letter that Kayla wrote to her parents from prison:

> I remember mom always telling me that all in all in the end the only one you really have is God. I have come to a place in experience where, in every sense of the word, I have surrendered myself to our creator [because] literally there was no else...[And] by God [and] by your prayers

> I have *felt tenderly cradled in freefall.* I have been shown in darkness, light [and] have learned that even in prison, one can be free...Please be patient[;] give your pain to God. I know you would want me to remain strong. That is exactly what I am doing. Do not fear for me, continue to pray as will I [and] by God's will we will be together soon. All my everything, Kayla.[21]

Notice that Kayla wrote that she "felt tenderly cradled in freefall."

French journalist Nicolas Henin, who was held in the same prison as Kayla, reported about a meeting that he and four other journalists had with Kayla. Henin said that Kayla "spent several months in isolation, and she—but she was impressive...I mean, she was strong inside. She obviously had been through some tough moments, but she managed very well to overcome them." When the Islamic British recruit and ISIS executioner called "Jihadi John believed that she converted to Islam[,] she said, 'Oh, I just want to correct you: I did not convert.' And, I mean, no one would dare to contradict him, but she did. That was not aggressive...she was just like that, very calm, but very decided."[22]

Kayla conquered.

Six months after Kayla was captured, three other women were imprisoned with her. One of them said of Kayla, "She had a strong faith that gave her a lot of strength."[23] Even when she had the chance to escape, Kayla put others first. A then thirteen-year-old Yazidi girl, who was a fellow prisoner, told Kayla that they were going to escape and asked Kayla to come with them. But Kayla "told me no, because I'm an American, if I escape with you they will do everything in their power to find you. It is better that you escape alone, I will stay here."[24]

Again, Kayla conquered.

Does it seem impossible to you, dear Christian, that Corrie ten Boom would write that in Ravensbrück "the life we lived with God, grew daily better, truth upon truth, glory upon glory," and that Kayla Mueller could write from prison that she "felt tenderly cradled in freefall"? Then consider Richard Wurmbrand, cofounder of The Voice of the Martyrs, who himself spent 13 years in communist prisons. Wurmbrand was for three years kept in complete solitary confinement and was often tortured and mutilated, yet he wrote:

> Often, after a secret service, Christians were caught and sent to prison. There, Christians wear chains with the gladness with which a bride wears a precious jewel received from her beloved. The waters in prison are still. They receive His kiss and His embraces, and would not change places with kings. I have found truly joyful Christians only in the Bible, in the Underground Church and in prison.[25]

"Truly joyful Christians" in prison? Corrie ten Boom, Kayla Mueller, and Richard Wurmbrand conquered.

So, dear Christian, let us commit ourselves to honoring God through whatever suffering the world and the devil throw at us, and we will be victorious conquerors who will be richly rewarded (much more about that in the final two chapters of this book).

CLAY'S STORY

In 2002, I (Clay) started experiencing lower back pain.[26] As the months went on, the pain increased, and I visited different doctors, all of whom told me that I needed to do stretching exercises (that is the remedy for many people's back pain). But my pain increased and became so severe that I could no longer sleep in my bed upstairs with Jean (this was very sad to me). I couldn't sleep well downstairs either, but at least I wasn't waking up Jean. Finally, I got a CT scan on a Friday morning, and the next Monday morning I got a phone call from my orthopedic surgeon. Not his nurse. Not an assistant. The doctor was on the phone, and I knew that meant it couldn't be good news.

The doctor told us (Jean was listening on another line) that I had "a mass" on my spine and that I needed to see a specialist who was located a long way from where we lived. After we hung up, I walked into Jean's home office and, with tears streaming down our faces, I thanked God for what He had allowed. At that moment, I knew that I had honored God in the face of extreme suffering, thus proving the sincerity of my faith. That didn't stop the tears (most of them in response to the prospect of me leaving Jean), but it did give me great comfort. My suffering had meaning. The heavenly host was watching, and I forced my mind to look to Jesus.

Then, the whirlwind began. Quickly I saw the specialist, who ordered a biopsy (which hurt, by the way). After the biopsy was done, we waited to hear the result. Finally, a few days later, my orthopedic oncologist told me that the lab diagnosed the biopsy as an aggressive form of cancer. First, he would treat it by chemo, and then, after six months or so, *if* the tumor shrank, he *might* opt to operate. But he also said he thought the biopsy results might be mistaken and he needed to see the slides himself. We were stunned. After we hung up, Jean and I met in the hallway. Again we held hands with tears streaming down our faces, and I led us in a prayer of thankfulness to God. Once again, I knew that I had demonstrated the reality of my faith to the Father and the heavenly host. I also knew that we had humiliated Satan.

I always emphasize the tears streaming down our faces because that's real—being faithful to God doesn't mean that we won't shed tears while we're being faithful. I forcefully chose to thank God regardless of my future on this earth, and that brought me a sense of honoring God amid great emotional and physical pain. That served as an anchor for our stormy lives.

As we said in the introduction, it's okay to mourn. Jesus says in

Matthew 5:4, "Blessed are those who mourn, for they shall be comforted." In Philippians 2:26-27, Paul writes that his brother and fellow soldier Epaphroditus has "been longing for you all and has been distressed because you heard that he was ill. Indeed he was ill, near to death. But God had mercy on him, and not only on him but on me also, lest I should have sorrow upon sorrow."

Note a couple of things. First, Paul didn't know whether God was going to heal Epaphroditus. Paul doesn't say, "But I prayed for Epaphroditus and, of course, God healed him because it is always God's will to heal." Rather, Paul writes that God had "mercy" upon them both. In Paul's mind it wasn't a given that Epaphroditus would be healed. Second, Paul writes that if God had not healed Epaphroditus, then Paul would have had "sorrow upon sorrow." It's okay to mourn. Sadly, some Christians want others not to mourn—at least not for very long. But the mourning process for losing someone you're close to, like a spouse, child, or parent, usually takes at least a year (or longer) because the person who has suffered the loss needs to experience every holiday, birthday, and so on at least once without their loved one's presence. But again, we can honor God through our tears and mourning.

Three years ago, when we first found out that I had cancer again, this time metastasized, we cried that night and much of the next day. But we honored God through it. Even through the tears, we thanked God for the suffering He allowed into our lives.

But we're thankful to report that the overwhelming majority of our days are rarely sad because, even as I have one procedure after another, we've learned to rely on seven truths to give us victory—the seven truths we will discuss in this book. We've found that when suffering strikes, regularly repeating and reflecting on these seven truths about suffering relieves our sadness and fears. We lived these truths in the past and we live them today. We can't emphasize this enough: *We live these truths and have experienced how they have blessed our lives.*

Of course, sometimes things get us down. But when that happens, we have learned that it makes all the difference to think through the seven truths and figure out which one or more of them we've lost sight of. For example, sometimes I will think of a negative possible future outcome and then may quickly put it out of my mind, but it's still roaming around in my subconscious and bringing me down. I then need to figure out what's bothering me. Asking, as David does in Psalm 42:5, "Why are you cast down, O my soul?" and then finding the answer makes a huge difference in our having peace and joy while suffering. If I realize that a negative possible future outcome is bothering me, then I recall that it may never happen (truth 5) and that even if it does happen, God loves us (truth 1) and He will work everything out for our good (truth 3).

Now, on to truth 1: God loves us.

2

TRUTH 1: GOD LOVES US

Clay: "The Lord loves Jean E. Jones and Clay B. Jones."

Jean: "Yes, the Lord does love Jean E. Jones and Clay B. Jones."

The chapters that follow begin with how we actually talk to each other. This may seem a little silly, even corny (and so it's a little embarrassing)—but we want to share how we apply these truths to give you a suggestion, dear reader, on how you might make it your own. For us, there's something about using our names that makes it more personal beyond just saying to each other, "God loves us." Also, Clay's present troubles with Afib and cancer affect both of us (sometimes what he's going through is even harder on Jean), and we both need encouragement.

Of course, one of us often isn't around and we realize that you may not have a willing spouse or intimate companion with whom to recite these truths. When we have sad thoughts but are alone, we turn these truths into prayers and recite them with the most intimate companions of all—Jesus and our heavenly Father. For example, when I (Clay) am alone during the day or tense thoughts interrupt my sleep, I'll pray something like "Thank You, Father, for loving me, and thank You, Jesus, for giving Your life for me," and I'll continue meditating on and rejoicing in God's love for me. In addition to reminding each other of these truths, we often turn this truth, and all the truths that follow, into prayers.

WHAT TO DO NOW: PRAY TO KNOW THE CENTRALITY OF THE TRUTH THAT GOD LOVES US

That God loves us, that He wants the best for us, and that He has the power to accomplish what is best for us is the foundation of all the subsequent truths. In Ephesians 3:17-19, Paul writes, "I pray that you, being rooted and established in love, may have power, together with all the Lord's holy people, to grasp how wide and long and high and deep is the love of Christ, and to know this love that surpasses knowledge—that you may be filled to the measure of all the fullness of God" (NIV). May we encourage you, dear reader, to pray Paul's prayer before you continue reading. We all need a revelation of the love of God.

GOD'S LOVE DISPLAYED THROUGH ABRAHAM AND ISAAC

In Jane Austen's *Pride and Prejudice*, Elizabeth Bennet spurns Mr. Darcy's marriage proposal despite his vast wealth and enviable social standing. Why? Because, she declares, Darcy ruined the romantic prospects of her sister and the financial prospects of Mr. Wickham, and these actions are proof of "your arrogance, your conceit, and your selfish disdain of the feelings of others."

The next day, however, she learns Darcy's motives. He had discouraged his friend from courting her sister mostly because she seemed indifferent toward the young man—and an embarrassed Elizabeth recalls she had been warned her sister was too guarded! More mortifying was the news that Wickham had rejected the clergyman livelihood he claimed Darcy had denied him, requesting and receiving money instead, and when he had gambled that away, he tried to elope with Darcy's 15-year-old sister to snag her inheritance. Only then do past discrepancies in Wickham's actions become clear to Elizabeth.

> "How despicably have I acted!" she cried; "I, who have prided myself on my discernment!...But vanity...has been my folly. Pleased with the preference of one, and offended by the neglect of the other...I have courted...ignorance, and driven reason away, where either were concerned."[1]

Understanding motives can make all the difference in our judgments of others. Genesis 22 tells the unsettling narrative of Abraham's near sacrifice of his son Isaac. The late author Rachel Held Evans posted a viral blog entitled "I would fail Abraham's test (and I bet you would too)." She writes, "I am not yet a mother, and still I know, deep in my gut, that I would sooner turn my back on everything I know to be true than sacrifice my child on the altar of religion."[2]

That a parent might sacrifice a child, even worse an only child, horrifies us.

And it should.

But before we get into the Lord's motives behind asking Abraham to offer Isaac as a sacrifice, we need some background. Earlier in Genesis, we see God had given Abraham tremendous evidence of His character and love. He had kept all His promises. He had performed many miracles for Abraham. Appearing to Abraham. Sending angels to Abraham. Helping him rescue his kidnapped nephew Lot by defeating the armies of four kings with only 318 men. Cutting a covenant with Abraham by passing a blazing torch and firepot between the two lines of animals that Abraham had sacrificed and laid out. But most importantly, promising Abraham a child through his barren wife, a promise God fulfilled when the postmenopausal Sarah was 91 years old, and Abraham was 100. They named the newborn boy Isaac. Of Isaac, God declared, "I will establish my covenant with him as an everlasting covenant for his offspring after him" (Genesis 17:19).

So Abraham knew God's character. He knew God was a loving promise keeper able and willing to do miracles. Thus, God had carefully prepared Abraham for His monumental request in Genesis 22.

There, God asks Abraham to take his son Isaac whom he loved to a mountain and offer him as a burnt offering. Abraham wouldn't have thought the request wrong. In Ur, where he came from, people believed human sacrifice was effective in manipulating fickle gods.[3] After all, if its inhabitants will die unless rain ends a famine, the one who offers himself or his child to save others will be honored.

It was a test, we're told. God asked tenderly. The word *now* in "Take now your son" (verse 2 NASB) is often translated "please" and has the sense of an entreaty. Professor Paul Copan says, "God's directive is unusual: '*Please* take your son'...God is remarkably gentle as he gives a difficult order. This type of divine command (as a plea) is rare."[4] But at the moment of no return, the angel of the Lord stops Abraham and shows him a ram to offer instead.

Why did God ask Abraham to do something He didn't intend for him to follow through on?

Let's look at what Scripture tells us were God's motives.

Motive 1: Proving Abraham Loved God

The story tells us one of the motives: It was a test that proved Abraham's devotion (Genesis 22:1, 12): "Now I know that you fear God." Most of Abraham's life was materially and spiritually blessed; his faithful passing of this test demonstrated unbought love. Now, his descendants could know they too could trust God, though they had less visible evidence than he. They would need this reassurance through the coming Egyptian captivity and other difficult times. Abraham's faith was realized and proven.

Motive 2: Showing God Didn't Want Humans Sacrificing Humans

In that moment, God stopping Abraham showed that He did not want humans sacrificing humans. Later, when God gave Moses the Law, He forbade human sacrifice (Leviticus 18:21; 20:2-5).

Motive 3: Preaching the Gospel to Abraham

Galatians 3:8 tells us that in this story of Abraham sacrificing Isaac, the Scripture foresaw "that God would justify the Gentiles [non-Jews] by faith" and "preached the gospel beforehand to Abraham." In other words, as Timothy George puts it, "The good news of salvation was to be extended to all peoples, including the Gentiles, who would be declared righteous by God, just like Abraham, on the basis of faith."[5]

So how did this story preach the gospel?

By Foreshadowing the Father Sacrificing Jesus

Abraham and Isaac were prophets.[6] Sometimes God asked prophets to be portents by performing actions that foreshadowed and explained future events.[7] The actions were often shocking so that they would be remembered when the future event occurred, and people would recognize the significance of the event and that it came from God. Hebrews 11:17-19 explains:

> By faith Abraham, when he was tested, offered up Isaac, and he who had received the promises was offering up his only begotten son; it was he to whom it was said, "In Isaac your descendants shall be called." He considered that God is able to raise people even from the dead, from which he also received him back as a type (NASB1995).

So Abraham receiving his son back through substitutionary sacrifice was a type of the Father receiving His Son back through resurrection. Consider the similarities between Isaac and Jesus:

- Isaac's and Jesus' births were both prophesied.
- Their births were both miraculous.
- They each carried the wood upon which they would be sacrificed.
- They willingly submitted to the offering of their bodies.

On this last point, there's something important that we shouldn't miss: When Abraham began to bind Isaac, Isaac understood he was the sacrifice. He was between 15 and 30 years old and was stronger and faster than his aged father, but he allowed Abraham to bind him and lay him down on the stack of wood.[8] Isaac participated willingly.

Thus, Abraham's near sacrifice of his willing son, Isaac, foreshadowed the Father sacrificing His willing Son, Jesus, to atone for human sins.

By Showing How God Would Fulfill His promises to Abraham

After the angel stopped Abraham from completing the sacrifice, God said, "In your offspring shall all the nations of the earth be blessed, because you have obeyed my voice" (Genesis 22:18). According to Galatians 3:16 and 19, this "offspring" is Jesus, and Jesus blessed "all the nations of the earth" by dying to pay the penalty for people's sins so that those who had faith in Him could be declared righteous.

By Foretelling Jesus' Substitutionary Provision

Just as the Lord God substituted a ram for Isaac, so would the Lord God substitute His Son as a sacrifice for others. Rightly, Abraham prophesied in Genesis 22:8, 14, "The Lord will provide."

Motive 4: Providing Evidence that Jesus' Crucifixion Was in His Plan

God preached the gospel to Abraham beforehand so that when Jesus died and rose again, Abraham's descendants might recognize the parallel and accept His work on the cross as from God. Jesus told the Jews, "For if you believed Moses, you would believe me; for he wrote of me" (John 5:46). This account of Abraham and Isaac is one of the places that the first five books of the Bible talk about Jesus.

But the evidence wasn't for Jews alone. God also gave this evidence so that non-Jews could see that saving humans through Jesus' sacrifice was *always* God's plan. Clay took hermeneutics from D.A. Carson who made a point that always stuck with him: If one were to remove a passage from the Bible, how would that change our understanding of Scripture?[9] Certainly, if the Abraham and Isaac story were removed from Scripture, it would weaken our understanding and appreciation of Jesus' death on the cross. It's important not to ignore any passage of Scripture but instead seek to understand its meaning in the overall context of Scripture.

Motive 5: Showing What God's Love Looks Like

The Passover lamb is another sign that points to Jesus' sacrifice. But an animal sacrifice doesn't come near to expressing the fullness of what the Father and Son were willing to do to save humankind. Abraham's sacrifice of Isaac does.

God was demonstrating exactly what His love for sinful people looks like: the Father sending His willing Son to die for humankind's sins.

The angel of the Lord stopped Abraham from sacrificing Isaac. But no one stayed the hand of the Father: "For God so loved the world, that He gave His only begotten Son, that whoever believes in Him shall not perish, but have eternal life" (John 3:16 NASB1995).

GOD'S LOVE DISPLAYED THROUGH JESUS

If you are a true Christian, God loves you! The trouble with telling people that God loves them is what Clay calls the blah-blah-blah factor. "I know, God loves me, blah, blah, blah." "We've all heard it before." But let's look deeper.

At the outset, it's essential to note that Jesus had a choice. Jesus *did not* have to die for our sins. Jesus says in John 10:17-18, "For this reason the Father loves me, because I lay down my life that I may take it up again. No one takes it from me, but I lay it down of my own accord. I have authority to lay it down, and I have authority to take it up again. This charge I have received from my Father."[10] Also, the night Jesus was arrested, we learn from Matthew 26:51-53 that one of those with Jesus drew a sword and cut off the high priest's servant's ear. To this Jesus replied, "Put your sword back into its place... Do you think that I cannot appeal to my Father, and he will at once send me more than twelve legions of angels?" A full Roman legion was 6,000, so that means that Jesus could have called down 72,000 angels for assistance if He wanted.[11] Remember that one angel killed 185,000 Assyrians in a single night (Isaiah 37:36), so Jesus certainly could have stopped His arrest and crucifixion if He wanted. Thus, Jesus went to the cross willingly. This was not divine child abuse. Rather, Jesus says in John 15:13, "Greater love has no one than this: to lay down one's life for one's friends" (NIV). Let's look at what Jesus endured to demonstrate His great love.

Jesus Humbled Himself at the Incarnation

In Philippians 2:6-8 we read that Jesus, "though he was in the form of God, did not count equality with God a thing to be grasped, but emptied himself, by taking the form of a servant, being born in the likeness of men. And being found in human form, he humbled himself by becoming obedient to the point of death, even death on a cross."

Jesus created everything that exists. Before the incarnation, He truly "had it all." But Jesus' transformation from the splendor of all-knowing, almighty God to becoming a human who dies for humankind was a huge demonstration of His love for His people.

Christians ask how Jesus could still be God and yet be subject to all the limitations of being a man. To adapt a great analogy by theologian Millard Erickson, imagine the "world's fastest sprinter is entered in a three-legged race" with his seven-year-old son where one of each of their legs is tied together. "Although his physical capacity is not diminished," the conditions under which he exercises it are severely hindered. Erickson points out that, "Even if his partner in the race is the world's second fastest sprinter, their time will be much slower than if they competed separately; for that matter, it will be slower than the time for almost any other human running unencumbered."[12] Likewise, the King of kings and Lord of lords gave up His most exalted position for us.[13] Jesus entered this world of hurt and hunger, disease and bile, of sickness and deformity, where He was mocked, stripped naked, and ultimately crucified, for us. He didn't have to, but He loved us.

Sorrow and Stress in Gethsemane

Some Christians say that what Jesus endured wouldn't have been that bad because Jesus is God, so He really wouldn't feel it. But that's not what Scripture teaches. Just a short time prior to Jesus' capture and crucifixion, while in the garden of Gethsemane, He told the disciples, "My soul is *overwhelmed with sorrow* to the point of death" (Matthew 26:38 NIV). Luke 22:41-44 continues the narrative:

> He withdrew from them about a stone's throw, and knelt down and prayed, saying, "Father, if you are willing, remove this cup from me. Nevertheless, not my will, but yours, be done." And there appeared to him an angel from heaven, strengthening him. And being *in agony* he prayed more earnestly; and *his sweat became like great drops of blood falling down* to the ground.

Sweating blood is a real thing. The *Journal of the American Medical Association* (*JAMA*) explains, "Although this is a very rare phenomenon, bloody sweat (hematidrosis or hemohidrosis) may occur in highly emotional states or in persons with bleeding disorders. As a result of hemorrhage into the sweat glands, the skin becomes fragile and tender. Luke's description supports the diagnosis of hematidrosis."[14] Thus, Jesus suffered immensely. (That sweating blood is a real thing is another reason that we should believe the truth of this account. That Jesus appeared to be "sweating blood" is an incidental, off-hand comment that's not the point of the narrative. It's more of a "by the way, His sweat looked like blood" comment that appears to be no more than mere reportage.)

Jesus endured this because God loves us.

Betrayed, Spit on, Struck, Slapped, and Mocked by the Jewish Council

It's famous that Judas betrayed Jesus, but that should not be taken lightly. Jean and I have both felt the sting of betrayal. You probably have too. There's something horrible about having someone you trust turn against you. After Jesus was arrested and stood before the Jewish council, "They spit in his face and struck him with their fists. Others slapped him and said, 'Prophesy to us, Messiah. Who hit you?' " (Matthew 26:67-68 NIV).

Stripped, Flogged, and Scourged

Then we learn that Pilate had Jesus flogged to appease the Jews without killing Him (John 19:1). This was likely the least severe form of flogging.[15] Later, Matthew 27:26 reports that Jesus was stripped and scourged, the most severe form of flogging:[16] "Then he released for them Barabbas, and having scourged Jesus, delivered him to be crucified."[17] *JAMA* explains:

> The usual instrument was a short whip...with several single or braided leather thongs of variable lengths, in

> which small iron balls or sharp pieces of sheep bones were tied at intervals…For scourging, the man was stripped of his clothing, and his hands were tied to an upright post. The back, buttocks, and legs were flogged either by two soldiers (lictors) or by one who alternated positions. The severity of the scourging depended on the disposition of the lictors and was intended to weaken the victim to a state just short of collapse or death…Then, as the flogging continued, the lacerations would tear into the underlying skeletal muscles and produce quivering ribbons of bleeding flesh. Pain and blood loss generally set the stage for circulatory shock.[18]

Jesus endured this because He loves us.

Stripped Again, Repeatedly Struck, and Mocked in Front of a Battalion

Matthew 27:27-30 reads:

> Then the soldiers of the governor took Jesus into the governor's headquarters, and they gathered the whole battalion before him. And they stripped him and put a scarlet robe on him, and twisting together a crown of thorns, they put it on his head and put a reed in his right hand. And kneeling before him, they mocked him, saying, "Hail, King of the Jews!" And they spit on him and took the reed and struck him on the head.

We have rose and bougainvillea plants in our yard. They are beautiful (well, roses are beautiful most of the year), but they also have many thorns. I (Clay) have been punctured many times by thorns, and I can hardly imagine having thorns made into a crown and pressed into my head.

Crucified Naked and Ridiculed

Matthew 27:31 says, "After they had mocked him, they took off the robe and put his own clothes on him. Then they led him away to crucify him" (NIV). Craig Blomberg points out that "Crucifixions were usually held alongside well-traveled roads to remind as many people as possible of the high cost of crime, particularly treason against the empire."[19]

In artistic renderings, Jesus is portrayed as having on a loin cloth, but that's for modesty's sake. John 19:23 tells us, "When the soldiers crucified Jesus, they took his clothes" (NIV). So the crucified Jesus was naked and would have to—dare I say it?—poop and pee as he excruciatingly pivoted on the spikes in His wrists to lift Himself up and down to keep from suffocating.[20]

It helps us understand the extent of God's love for us if we fully grasp what it meant for Jesus to be crucified. And it helps those who have suffered humiliating abuse to know that Jesus suffered like they did.

JAMA tells us, "Not uncommonly, insects would light upon or burrow into the open wounds or the eyes, ears, and nose of the dying and helpless victim, and birds of prey would tear at these sites." While this was going on, to exhale, Jesus would have to lift His body by pushing up on His feet, which would place the entire weight of His body on the pierced bones of His feet, which would "produce searing pain." Further, Jesus would have to rotate His "wrists about the iron nails," which would cause "fiery pain." Lifting His body would also scrape His scourged back against the cross's wooden post and would result in muscle cramps. *JAMA* continues, "As a result, each respiratory effort would become agonizing and tiring and lead eventually to asphyxia."[21] In other words, most victims of crucifixions eventually suffocated because they could no longer lift themselves to breathe. This could take hours, or even days, depending on their physical state. Flogging and scourging had already weakened Jesus, as was seen by the fact that He couldn't carry the crossbar of His cross (Matthew 27:32), which weighed between 75 and 125 pounds.[22]

I (Clay) have endured a lot of painful procedures at the hands of medical professionals—sometimes very painful procedures. But while undergoing these hardships I've often considered that the medical professionals inflicting the pain were trying to help me. They were trying to make my life better. But those torturing Jesus were only out to hurt Him. Their goal was to inflict pain. That's a whole different level of suffering.

Jesus endured this because He loves us.

Then to literally add insult to injury, while Jesus was crucified, people ridiculed Him. "Those who passed by derided him," wagged their heads, and said, "You who would destroy the temple and rebuild it in three days, save yourself! If you are the Son of God, come down from the cross" (Matthew 27:39-40). The chief priests, with the scribes and elders, also mocked Him: "He saved others; he cannot save himself. He is the King of Israel; let him come down now from the cross, and we will believe in him. He trusts in God; let God deliver him now, if he desires him. For he said, 'I am the Son of God'" (verses 41-43). Even the robbers crucified with Him reviled Him (verse 44).

Jesus endured this because God loves us.

Felt Abandoned by the Father

The worst horror of all is that Jesus sensed being abandoned by His Father. Matthew 27:46 reads, "About the ninth hour Jesus cried out with a loud voice, '*Eli, Eli, lema sabachthani*?' that is, 'My God, my God, why have you forsaken me?'" There are a lot of theories about what Jesus exactly experienced, but D.A. Carson is right: "It is better to take the words at face value: Jesus is conscious of being abandoned by his Father. For one who knew the intimacy of Matthew 11:27, such an abandonment must have been agony; and for the same reason, it is inadequate to hypothesize that Jesus felt abandoned but was not truly abandoned..."[23] Carson quotes Douglas Moo: "It seems difficult to understand how Jesus, who had lived in the closest possible fellowship with the Father, could have been unaware whether he had, in fact, been abandoned..."[24] Blomberg writes that Jesus "apparently senses an abrupt loss of the communion with the Father which had proved so intimate and significant throughout his life."[25] Carson personalizes this, "Jesus cried, 'My God, I am forsaken!' so that for all eternity Don Carson would not have to—'That, of the lost, no son should use those words of desolation!' "[26]

Died and Was Buried

Have you ever thought about your burial after you die? Someone will probably strip you naked, clean you up, and dress you again. That's icky. I (Clay) really don't want people—even though they may be trying to help—giving my dead body a bath. I told Jean that I don't want an open casket at my funeral. I don't care if seeing my dead body would help people with their grieving process! They'll just have to get over it.

Jesus died for us because God loves us.

When people challenge God's goodness—why a good God would allow this or that type of suffering into someone's lives—I often respond that whatever you think of God's goodness, let's remember that our heavenly Father sent His Son, Jesus, to be stripped naked, scourged, and impaled, hanging on spikes driven through His hands and feet until He died. Jesus did this to demonstrate God's love for us and to show His desire that we be forgiven of our sins and have eternal life with Him. Jesus' death and resurrection are the ultimate proof of God's love for us. They are the foundation of the truth of Christianity. That's why Paul writes in Romans 5:7-8, "Very rarely will anyone die for a righteous person, though for a good person someone might possibly dare to die. But God demonstrates his own love for us in this: While we were still sinners, Christ died for us" (NIV). God used

Jesus' suffering and death to pay for our sins and so give those who trust in Him eternal life with Him. Thus, when we find ourselves uncertain about the future, we remind each other that God loves us.

And that brings us to our next truth. Unless one dies suddenly, everyone will suffer and face the prospect of their deaths.

3

TRUTH 2: EVERYONE IS GOING TO GO THROUGH THIS

Clay: "Everyone is going to go through this."

Jean: "Everyone."

Remembering that we are not alone helps put our problems into perspective. The Bible is filled with examples of godly people who suffer. Moses spent 40 years in the wilderness with a rebellious people; Job's family was killed and painful boils afflicted him; Joseph's brothers sold him into slavery; David spent ten years running from the murderous King Saul; and Paul, among many other sufferings, was stoned. So it shouldn't surprise us when we too suffer. After all, as we mentioned in the introduction, the only thing that is going to prevent us from watching everyone we know die from murder, accident, or disease will be our own deaths from murder, accident, or disease. Indeed, we live in a fallen world and must understand that suffering is God's plan for us—but eternal glory awaits!

THE BAD NEWS

Twenty-three years ago, when I (Clay) was first diagnosed with bone cancer, I walked down a hospital office-building corridor on my way to get my first MRI. I'm not a morning person and it was early—a dark, drizzly, and cold January morning. The hospital hallway looked ugly, and I asked the Lord, "Why me?" I wasn't complaining—honestly. I simply wanted to know why I, at 47 years old, was in immense pain from bone cancer. Immediately the words came to mind, "Everyone is going to go through this." It may seem strange, but I found that comforting. I wasn't alone. God wasn't picking on or overlooking me. Rather, everyone is going to go through this. Maybe not bone cancer, but, as we said, unless we die suddenly, we're all going to walk down a doctor's office corridor wondering if we're going to get potentially life-ending news.[1] It might be cancer, heart disease, dementia, or whatever, but everyone is going to go through this.

Over a photo of the 1533 Lucas Cranach painting of Eve handing Adam an apple out of which she had already taken a bite, *The Babylon Bee* placed the headline, "Couple Follows Their Hearts; Billions Dead."[2] That's my favorite *Babylon Bee* headline because it's funny, true, and staggering in its implications. Adam and Eve's sin is the near origin of our earthly sufferings, but the ultimate origin of our suffering goes further back. Much further.

We submit to you that every accident, maiming, cold, cancer, torture, murder, form of dementia, *ad infinitum, ad nauseam* began a long, long time ago with a single angelic grumble in heaven. After all, every human rebellion begins with a grumble. One person grumbles to another person that this or that teacher, boss, principal, mayor, ruler, king, or president treats us unfairly (which may or may not be true). They think, *We deserve better!* If the first grumbler gathers a few fellow grumblers, and then a few more, then, sooner or later, this results in covert rebellion—or if the grumblers think they can pull it off, in overt rebellion that leads to actions like walkouts, strikes, or even open warfare.

We know that Satan rebelled and took many angels with him. Their rebellion almost certainly began with a grumble that God was holding them back from something good, from something that might benefit them. Satan succeeded in getting other angels to agree that God wasn't acting in their best interest and therefore, in some way, wasn't good. They thought that they should have more than what God was giving them. Once the grumbling turned into actual rebellion, the war was on. This is described in Isaiah 14:12-14:

> How you are fallen from heaven,
> O Day Star, son of Dawn!
> How you are cut down to the ground,
> you who laid the nations low!
> You said in your heart,
> "I will ascend to heaven;
> above the stars of God
> I will set my throne on high;
> I will sit on the mount of assembly
> in the far reaches of the north;
> I will ascend above the heights of the clouds;
> I will make myself like the Most High."[3]

There it is: Satan said in his heart that he would make himself like God. We find a similar boast in Ezekiel 28:2: "Your heart is proud, and you have said, 'I am a god.'"[4]

Sometime after Satan and his minions rebelled, the Lord created hell for them (Matthew 25:41). So what's a devil to do? Well, what do all humans do—especially politicians—when they are caught doing something evil? If they can, they point to others who have also done evil: "See, they do it too!" It started with Satan, who is engaged in the ultimate "what-aboutism." Satan complains that others are similarly evil. The word *satan* means adversary or accuser. And indeed, Revelation 12:10 says that Satan is the "accuser of our brothers" and that he "accuses them day and night before our God."[5] What's Satan's point? It's that if Satan couldn't keep God's laws, then neither can anyone else. And if that's the case, then God demands too much of His creatures. God asks too much of us; He sets the bar too high.

When the Bible talks about Christians suffering for Jesus' sake or for righteousness' sake, we typically consider it to be referring to physical suffering inflicted by other humans. While that is often the case, remember that Satan and his minions may also use accident or disease to persecute righteous Christians, as he did with Job. Job 2:3-8 reads,

> The LORD said to Satan, "Have you considered my servant Job, that there is none like him on the earth, a blameless and upright man, who fears God and turns away from evil? He still holds fast his integrity, although you incited me against him to destroy him without reason." Then Satan answered the LORD and said, "Skin for skin! All that a man has he will give for his life. But stretch out your hand and touch his bone and his flesh, and he will curse you to your face." And the LORD said to Satan, "Behold, he is in your hand; only spare his life."
>
> So Satan went out from the presence of the LORD and struck Job with loathsome sores from the sole of his foot to the crown of his head. And he took a piece of broken pottery with which to scrape himself while he sat in the ashes.

What's Satan's motive? He wants to besmirch the Lord by claiming that the Lord sets the bar too high; the Lord demands too much of us. In other words, Satan wants to proclaim that God isn't good (thus the so-called "problem of evil" about which Clay has written a book).[6] Indeed, as G.K. Beale puts it: "Until the death of Christ, it could appear that the devil had a good case, since God ushered all deceased OT saints into his saving presence without exacting the penalty of their sin. Satan was allowed to lodge these complaints because there was some degree of truth in them."[7] But once Jesus honored God, despite immense suffering, He justified Satan's judgment and Satan's case was lost. Thus, Revelation 12:10 says, "Now the salvation and the power and the kingdom of our God and the authority of his Christ have come, for the accuser of our brothers has been thrown down, who accuses them day and night before our God." Then, in the next verse it says about us, "And they have conquered him by the blood of the Lamb and by the word of their testimony, for they loved not their lives even unto death." So Satan brings suffering into our lives to try to get us to dishonor God. But when we honor God through suffering, we too justify the judgment of Satan and his minions and conquer them.

After all, that was exactly Satan's contention to Eve in the garden. Eve told Satan that if they ate from the tree of the knowledge of good and evil, they would die. But Satan replied, "You will not surely die. For God knows that when you eat of it your eyes will be opened, and you will be *like God*, knowing good and evil" (Genesis 3:4-5). Satan was saying that God was holding back Adam and Eve from something that would otherwise benefit them (not getting what you want is a type of suffering). Satan was saying that God, by forbidding that fruit, wasn't acting in their best interest. In other words, Satan claimed that God is not good—He asks too much of us.

Eve succumbed to Satan's wiles, Adam joined her, and God then cursed the ground (Genesis 3:17), which enabled every kind of natural evil from colds to cancers. God kicked the man and woman out of the garden of Eden, and we've been attending funerals ever since. Then Adam and Eve had kids who had kids, and so on, and here we are in this world of immense suffering where everyone eventually dies. Thankfully, a time when there will be no more death or mourning or crying or pain will come—in a place the Old and New Testaments most often compare to a banquet.

But here we suffer.

I (Clay) have interviewed four Navy SEALs, and one of them told me that the Christian's life is more emotionally demanding than becoming a Navy SEAL because, unlike SEAL training, the Christian's training ends 100 percent of the time in our own death. It's also not uncommon for the Christian's life to be more physically demanding than Navy SEAL training because not only do most Christians need to endure debilitating diseases (if they live long enough), many Christians are tortured to death precisely because they are Christians. As Jesus says in Matthew 24:9-13:

> Then they will deliver you up to tribulation and put you to death, and you will be hated by all nations for my name's sake. And then many will fall away and betray one another and hate one another. And many false prophets will arise and lead many astray. And because lawlessness will be increased, the love of many will grow cold. But the one who endures to the end will be saved.

We Christians are going to suffer (so are non-Christians, by the way), but we need to honor Jesus and focus on eternity.

When we (Clay and Jean) say to each other, "Everyone is going to go through this," we aren't referring to particular aspects of what any one individual is suffering. We mean that sooner or later, unless a person dies young and suddenly, everyone is going to go through a lot of suffering and get a debilitating disease or injury that *will* kill them—and that includes every Christian.

First Corinthians 10:13 tells us, "No temptation has overtaken you that is not common to man. God is faithful, and he will not let you be tempted beyond your ability, but with the temptation he will also provide the way of escape, that you may be able to endure it." Notice: "common to man." Paul is saying that when you suffer, you are not alone. When we received Clay's most recent cancer diagnosis, I (Jean) began reminding myself regularly that most married women must face what I'm facing: the prospect of a husband dying.

It's important to note that the Greek word for "temptation" in this verse is *peirasmos,* and that is the same word commonly translated "trial" in the New Testament (e.g., James 1:2, 12). Douglas Moo writes that the use of the word in the James passages "refers to any difficulty in life that may threaten our faithfulness to Christ: physical illness, financial reversal, the death of a loved one."[8] Suffering is always a trial *and* a temptation—it tests our faith and tempts us to not trust God.

Peter writes something similar to "common to man" (1 Corinthians 10:13) in 1 Peter 4:12-13: "Beloved, do not be surprised at the fiery trial when it comes upon you to test [*peirasmos*] you, as though something strange were happening to you. But rejoice insofar as you share Christ's sufferings, that you may also rejoice and be glad when his glory is revealed."

Once again, "fiery ordeal" and glory appear together. Consider that if God won't allow us to be tried or tempted beyond what we are able to resist, then in what sense can't we handle those trials or temptations? God won't give us more than we can handle. Further, we should "not be surprised at the fiery trial" that comes upon us.

Jesus encourages us in Matthew 10:29-31 that even though "two sparrows" are "sold for a penny," nonetheless, "not one of them will fall to the ground apart from your Father. But even the hairs of your head are all numbered. Fear not, therefore; you are of more value than many sparrows." Thus, we can have confidence that every suffering that comes upon us is in accord with the Father's will.

Now, if your life is presently easy and your future looks bright, "we are all going to go through this" is less likely to comfort you. We were having dinner with a couple of good friends at a steakhouse, and Clay mentioned how the two of us are comforted by the fact that everyone is going to go through what we're going through. But the wife said, "That doesn't comfort me" (because at that moment their lives were pleasant). Of course, when your life is comfortable, you're not going to be happy that everyone is going to suffer. But it does comfort those who are presently suffering.

Dealing with Difficult Emotions

As I (Jean) mentioned in chapter 1, when I prayed, "But everyone else can have kids. Why can't I?" I immediately recognized my foolishness. Of course that wasn't true. But false beliefs like this one can lurk like hidden sharks beneath the deep waters of our thoughts. From there they whip up difficult emotions like anger and depression that then swirl to the surface. When faced with difficult emotions, we've learned the value of praying to uncover their source.

Pray Honestly

Psalm 42 is a great example of how to pray when emotions get crazy.[9] In it, the psalmist takes his true feelings, beliefs, and questions to God in prayer. When we pray honestly, the Holy Spirit often reveals the truths we need. Perhaps we'll sense the truth immediately. Or the next time we pick up the Bible, the verse we need will jump out at us. Maybe we'll hear a sermon or talk to a friend who has the message we need.

Here is how Psalm 42:1-6, 8 teaches us to pray honestly.

Tell God the problem: "As a deer pants for flowing streams, so pants my soul for you, O God. My soul thirsts for God, for the living God. When shall I come and appear before God?" (verses 1-2). Like the psalmist, we can cry out to God and tell Him how much we long for Him and need Him.

Honestly describe our emotions: "My tears have been my food day and night, while they say to me all the day long, 'Where is your God?' " (verse 3). We can tell God what we are feeling.

Remember past times when we felt God's presence: "These things I remember, as I pour out my soul: how I would go with the throng and lead them in procession to the house of God with glad shouts and songs of praise, a multitude keeping festival" (verse 4). The psalmist remembers past times when he felt God's presence. Recalling God's prior care gives us hope for His present and future care.

Ask ourselves why we're troubled: "Why are you cast down, O my soul, and why are you in turmoil within me?" (verse 5). When we're down, we often ask ourselves this question in similar words. Identifying the cause of our sadness is important so that we can address it directly. In verses 9-10, the psalmist answers his question: enemies oppress and taunt him. Here are examples of how we might express our emotions:

- *I'm angry that I didn't get the promotion I deserved. My pride is wounded, and my ambitions are blocked.*
- *God hasn't answered my prayers, and I wonder if He cares about me.*
- *I'm discouraged and wonder what's wrong with me that I can't find a job. I wonder if God is mad at me.*
- *I miss my loved one so much since their death, and it's hard to imagine being happy without them.*

Tell ourselves to hope in God: "Hope in God; for I shall again praise him, my salvation and my God" (verses 5-6). The psalmist reminds himself to hope in God, for this hardship will pass and he'll praise God on the other side. Here are encouragements we might give ourselves:

- *Hope in God, for I will see that His plans for me are good. He's purging selfish ambitions and will lift me up when I humble myself.*
- *Hope in God, for He cares for me deeply and sorrows over my pain, and I will look back and see His loving hand.*
- *Hope in God, for I will look back and see how He was guiding me to the right job.*
- *Hope in God, for I will look back and praise Him for how He cared for me and brought me companions, and I will reunite with my loved one in heaven.*

Confess trust in God: "By day the Lord commands his steadfast love, and at night his song is with me, a prayer to the God of my life" (verse 8). We can pray verse 8 simply as it is.

WHAT TO DO NOW: UNCOVER THE SOURCE OF DIFFICULT EMOTIONS

This week, you might try this: Every time you feel sad or disturbed, stop and ask yourself this, "Why are you cast down, O my soul, and why are you in turmoil within me?" As soon as you identify the source of your emotions, remember God's promises related to your problem and imagine being on the other side. Then encourage yourself, "Hope in God; for I shall again praise him, my salvation and my God" (verse 11).

Embrace Truth

Uncovering the source of difficult emotions may reveal grief, shame, or heartbreak. But it may also uncover false beliefs. When we discover false beliefs, it's important to replace them with truth.

As we said before and will say again, we list truths that combat lies and truths that comfort us in our truth journals.

Law 1 of Cru's "The Four Spiritual Laws" is "God loves you and offers a wonderful plan for your life."[10] While that's true in the sense that once you become a Christian you know peace with God, have the forgiveness of your sins, and have the hope of eternal life, a lot of Christians also take that as meaning that you will have an improved lifestyle *here and now*. For example, if a Muslim converts to Christianity in Afghanistan, and his daughter is abducted, raped, and forced to sign a confession to Islam, and then the Taliban seeks to set him on fire, that's not an improved lifestyle *here and now*!

It's ironic how often people are surprised at encountering difficulties considering the Bible tells us they're the norm. As Moses writes, "The years of our life are seventy, or even by reason of strength eighty; yet their span is but toil and trouble; they are soon gone, and we fly away" (Psalm 90:10). Life on this earth is often troublesome, but it's also brief (although it doesn't seem so when we're young). Both the Old and New Testaments remind us to expect our lives to be short like grass in a field that withers and dies after flowering (see Psalms 37:2; 90:5-6; 103:15-16; Isaiah 40:6-8; 1 Peter 1:24).

But life's brevity blesses believers by removing them from earth's troubles: "The righteous man perishes, and no one lays it to heart; devout men are taken away, while no one understands. For the righteous man is taken away from calamity; he enters into peace; they rest in their beds who walk in their uprightness" (Isaiah 57:1-2).

Like Moses, Jesus warns His disciples that suffering will come: "I have said these things to you, that in me you may have peace. In the world you will have tribulation. But take heart; I have overcome the world" (John 16:33). In other words, knowing ahead of time that tough times await would give them peace when trials came. And they can be heartened that Jesus has overcome the world with its sin problem and is taking His followers to be with Him.

After the apostle Paul was stoned and left for dead, he and Barnabas traveled from city to city, "strengthening the souls of the disciples, encouraging them to continue in the faith, and saying that through many tribulations we must enter the kingdom of God" (Acts 14:22). They "strengthened" disciples by saying we must go through "many tribulations."

Embracing the truth that everyone suffers brings peace to sufferers.

We all must face the loss of loved ones and our own impending death. "It is appointed for man to die once, and after that comes judgment" (Hebrews 9:27). But that's also a comfort, for death is the passageway to heaven.

And that brings us to the good news.

THE GOOD NEWS

We may all be subject to sin, suffering, and death, "But God, being rich in mercy, because of the great love with which he loved us, even when we were dead in our trespasses, made us alive together with Christ—by grace you have been saved—and raised us up with him" (Ephesians 2:4-6). Those of us in Christ are alive in Christ right now. In John 8:51, Jesus says, "Truly, truly, I say to you, if anyone keeps my word, he will never see death." By using "truly, truly," Jesus is making a divine "listen up" statement. Pay attention! Then He says that those who keep His word "will never see death." Jesus isn't in denial. He isn't pretending that our bodies won't die. He is saying that our souls won't die. What is most fundamental and most essential about us won't die.

Similarly, in Luke 21:16-18, Jesus tells His disciples, "You will be delivered up even by parents and brothers and relatives and friends, and some of you they will put to death. You will be hated by all for my name's sake. But not a hair of your head will perish." Of course, many Christians, even in the last few years, have been beheaded or burned to death precisely because they were Christians, but Jesus says, "Not a hair of your head will perish." What Jesus means is that your most essential you—your soul and spirit—is going to go on regardless of what happens to your physical body. When your *body* does die, your consciousness will continue into what is now the unseen realm. Your consciousness won't even momentarily go dark. It won't be like a computer rebooting. Rather, your transition into the unseen realm will be so smooth, so seamless, so natural, that it may take you a while to realize that you've died.

We Christians who suffer together share an immediate sense of fellowship and bonding. We have something in common that we will take with us forever. Consider that those of us Christians who live on planet Earth, who suffer and ultimately die, will forever share that we were once in this world of toil and tears. After all, those who have gone through extremely difficult circumstances together—for example, D-Day—share a camaraderie, a fellowship from which those who didn't endure such hardships are excluded. Battle veterans often glory in the hardship shared in a conflict, and soldiers like thinking they did their *share* during a war.[11] And we Christians who have endured this world of suffering and death will throughout eternity have that in common.

In addition, there is something else Christians share right now. In our common fight against sin, we better understand our Lord. The Bible teaches that it is a privilege for the Christian to suffer for the cause of Christ: "It has been *granted* to you on behalf of Christ not only to believe in him, but also to suffer for him" (Philippians 1:29 NIV). It has been "granted" to us to share in the suffering of Christ. Peter writes that Christians should not be surprised at the painful trials they suffer but should rejoice that they "participate in the sufferings of Christ" (1 Peter 4:12-13 NIV). This sense of privilege in suffering is common to human experience.

As already mentioned in chapter one, we (Clay and Jean) weren't able to have children, so we took in neglected and abused foster children. At one time, we had three preteen/teenage girls. Sometimes the girls could be very rude, and after one dinner I (Clay) left our house and took a short walk down our street into an area where new houses were under construction. We had put up with a lot of rudeness and rebellion (we had the police at our house seven times in two-and-a-half years—it's always an event when the police are at your house), and it made me sad to think that maybe none of these girls would come to know Jesus. So I prayed, "Lord, what if none of these girls comes to know You?" Immediately the words came to mind, "Then you will know the fellowship of My suffering." That comforted me, and I considered how hard it must be on the Lord to have sent His Son to die for the world and yet have most of the world reject Him. Through what we were going through, I understood a little better how our Lord must feel. In that comforting phrase, I was recalling Paul's words that he wanted to "know Him and the power of His resurrection and the fellowship of His sufferings, being conformed to His death; if somehow I may attain to the resurrection from the dead" (Philippians 3:10-11 NASB). Not only is our suffering and death something that we will all endure, Jesus has that in common with us! Indeed, in Isaiah 53:3, we read about Jesus: "He was despised and rejected by men, a man of sorrows and acquainted with grief; and as one from whom men hide their faces he was despised, and we esteemed him not." Thus, when the world slanders and rejects us for being Christians, we will better understand our Lord.

But there's so much more! Yes, here on planet Earth we all share in suffering and death, but it doesn't end here. As we continue to honor God through suffering, our bodies may die, but we will then go on in a glorious eternity. We read in Ephesians 2:6 that "God raised us up with Christ and seated us with him in the heavenly realms in Christ Jesus" (NIV). Those of us who are "in Christ" are raised with

Christ and are actually "seated" with Christ in the heavenly realms presently, with the fuller realization of this coming at His return. We can say that we are presently seated with Christ because we are *in* Him and Christ lives in us (Galatians 2:20). There is an organic union between us.[12]

As Paul continues in Ephesians 2:6-7, God "raised us up with him and seated us with him in the heavenly places in Christ Jesus, so that in the coming ages he might show the immeasurable riches of his grace in kindness toward us in Christ Jesus." Peter T. O'Brien writes that "in the coming ages" means "one age supervening upon another like successive waves of the sea, as far into the future as thought can reach."[13] Do we see that there is an eternal lesson here? What God is doing among us suffering and physically dying Christians is something that will be used to teach nonhuman creatures (such as angels) in the ages to come. What a privilege; what an honor; what glory; what fulfillment! We all need to be a part of something bigger than ourselves, and this is as big as it gets. Throughout eternity God is going to use our exaltation as an object lesson of His grace "expressed in his kindness to us" as we are forever "seated" with Christ.

WHAT TO DO NOW: REJOICE IN THE LORD

Pray Philippians 4:4-6 segment by segment: "Rejoice in the Lord always; again I will say, rejoice. Let your reasonableness be known to everyone. The Lord is at hand; do not be anxious about anything, but in everything by prayer and supplication with thanksgiving let your requests be made known to God." Write the passage on a card or in a note on your smartphone so you can carry it with you until you've memorized it. Examples of how to do this follow below.

Find Comfort by Rejoicing

One of the things we have done whenever we've become sad over this or that prospect is to pray Philippians 4:4-6 out loud together:[14] "Rejoice in the Lord always; again I will say, rejoice. Let your reasonableness be known to everyone. The Lord is at hand; do not be anxious about anything, but in everything by prayer and supplication with thanksgiving let your requests be made known to God."

Paul was in prison as he wrote those words encouraging believers to rejoice always. Clay and I have taken these words to heart, especially in difficult circumstances. When we first received Clay's latest cancer diagnosis, we prayed Philippians 4:4-6 together at least once a day. We also both prayed it during our private prayer times. During calmer times, we pray it less frequently, though I (Jean) still aim to pray it at least once per week.

What's paradoxical is how praying these verses comforts us. Indeed, the next verse promises, "And the peace of God, which surpasses all understanding, will guard your hearts and your minds in Christ Jesus" (Philippians 4:7). Rejoicing in God's past good care assures me of His present and future good care.

Here is an abbreviated example of how we pray Philippians 4:4-6 together aloud (sometimes I begin, sometimes Clay begins):

> *Clay*: " 'Rejoice in the Lord always; again I will say, rejoice.' Father, I thank You for writing our names in the Book of Life. I thank You that we are going to live together forever and ever."
>
> *Jean:* "Lord, thank You for salvation. Thank You for the way You brought me to You when I was mixed up and lost. I rejoice in all the blessings You've poured into our lives. Thank You that You love us and are working all things out for our good. Thank You for bringing skilled doctors to us. I rejoice in the glorious inheritance that awaits us."

Clay: "'Let your reasonableness/gentleness be known to everyone.' Please help us, dear Father, to be humble examples of godliness to Your people."

Jean: "Yes, Lord, help us to show forbearance in all things so we glorify You. Let our actions be reasonable in light of Your promises."

Clay: "'The Lord is at hand.' We thank You, Father, that You are within our hand's reach. We thank You that You are present with us right now."

Jean: "Thank You that You are right here with us."

Clay: "'Do not be anxious about anything, but in everything by prayer and supplication with thanksgiving let your requests be made known to God.' Lord, this is hard on Jean and me, and we ask that the next procedure would go smoothly. Thank You for taking care of us and that You are working all these hard things out for our good."

Jean: "Father, I confess that I've been anxious about this upcoming procedure. Forgive me for that. I ask that You guide the doctor's hands so that the procedure goes well and no nerves are damaged. Thank You that all this is in Your hands. We trust You."

The first part of the prayer, rejoicing, is the longest part as we rejoice over as many blessings as we can recall. As we remember the wonderful things God has done for us and the glorious future that awaits, peace assures our hearts. When we ask for help in showing reasonableness to all, we recall our purpose, and that gives us hope. Picturing the Lord being "at hand" reassures us and reminds us He went through much worse and sympathizes with us. Praying with thanksgiving lets us request our heart's desires all the while assured that God works everything for our good.

And that is our next truth: God always works everything out for our good.

4

TRUTH 3, PART 1: GOD WILL WORK EVERYTHING OUT FOR OUR GOOD

Clay: "God always works every hard thing out for our good."

Jean: "Always."

Clay: "Every hard thing."

Jean: "He always has, and He always will."

In this chapter, we share stories of how God has worked suffering for good in our own lives. Each vignette starts with a verse related to how God uses suffering for good. In the next chapter, we'll delve more deeply into what the Bible teaches about how God uses suffering in every Christian's life.

SUFFERING TEACHES AND GIFTS: CHILDLESSNESS

We know that for those who love God all things work together for good, for those who are called according to his purpose.

ROMANS 8:28

I (Jean) expected not to see many reasons during my life for why God chose the path of childlessness for me. With "Why?" in the box, I no longer looked for answers.

But the passing years have shown it to be a good path. It showed me that God doesn't want us to have blind faith, but rather faith that sees hardship clearly and still trusts God. It brought a better understanding of how God's deep love for us requires that He allow us to suffer to become conformed to Christ's image.

This is clear in Jeremiah. Many people quote Jeremiah 29:11 as if it were a promise that only good things will happen to us: "For I know the plans I have for you, declares the Lord, plans for welfare and not for evil, to give you a future and a hope." But verse 10 names the plans: The Lord was exiling His people to vicious Babylon for 70 years. They didn't think that plan was good. Indeed, Babylon burned the temple and palace, dashed their infants on rocks, thrust through the elderly, and chained starving survivors together for a long march to exile. There they lamented, "O God, why do you cast us off forever? Why does your anger smoke against the sheep of your pasture?" (Psalm 74:1). The answer: Temporary exile was the only way to bring the people back to their purpose of being God's people, for they had strayed far away (Jeremiah 2:25; 30:12-13).

Hearing that some church friends blamed my miscarriages on a lack of faith forced me to care less about what others said and more about what God says. Scripture commands this, but the only way to grow in this is to go through times that require such growth (see John 5:44; 1 Corinthians 4:1-5; Galatians 1:10). However, this turned out to be but the first step toward strengthening a major area of weakness.

Childlessness brought opportunities for special ministries. For example, I was able to minister to other childless women. Women came to me with their struggles because they knew I'd similarly suffered. I had time to lead women's groups, volunteer at church, write Bible studies, and teach. But perhaps most importantly, if Clay and I had had our own children, we wouldn't have been able to take in abandoned and abused children who couldn't be placed in families with other children.

Amazingly, I can honestly say the blessings have already been more than worth the hardships.

SUFFERING WELL MATURES: REMEMBERING PAST DELIVERANCES ENCOURAGES GREATLY

Not only that, but we rejoice in our sufferings, knowing that suffering produces endurance, and endurance produces character, and character produces hope.

ROMANS 5:3-4

Jean just shared how God's past deliverance through childlessness became a blessing for her. Indeed, few things encourage us more than remembering past deliverances. All true Christians will endure suffering. But when the Lord brings us out of it, seeing how He used that suffering for our good encourages us. Now if you haven't been walking closely with Jesus for very long, then you might not have a past deliverance to encourage you, but in time you'll see the Lord bring you into periods of suffering and you will see how God used them for your good.

Both of us list the ways God has blessed us and the ways He's worked hardship out for our good in our truth journals. Jean lists what she just shared in her truth journal. On tough days with disappointing news, we read over these pages and are encouraged. We encourage you, dear reader, to make such a list for yourself. We explain how in chapter 5.

SUFFERING GIVES ASSURANCE, BOLDNESS, AND SELF-CONTROL: THE UNPARDONABLE SIN

We destroy arguments and every lofty opinion raised against the knowledge of God, and take every thought captive to obey Christ.

2 CORINTHIANS 10:5

I (Clay) became a Christian two days before my thirteenth birthday at a Billy Graham crusade, and in a few months, I was reading the Bible about three hours a day, every day. I couldn't get enough of it! I was a terribly insecure, undisciplined high school freshman with a 1.9 GPA. I basically learned to read by reading the Bible. Then, a few months before I turned 15, my first major trial struck: I thought that I had committed the unpardonable sin of the blasphemy of the Holy Spirit. To say I was deeply distressed is an understatement. My parents took me to several pastoral counselors who assured me that I was misunderstanding passages like Matthew 12:32 and that I hadn't committed the unpardonable sin. But after I left their offices, I thought, *What if they're wrong and I really did commit the blasphemy of the Holy Spirit?* Every time I thought I had assured myself that I hadn't committed it, a contrary thought would again threaten me. I kept engaging in this intellectual battle. I felt like I was playing intellectual chess with the devil, and he always won.

I got over it by typing out the verses that promised my guaranteed salvation, and whenever I thought that I was lost, I would quote those verses to myself in a loop until I felt better.[1] Quoting those verses brought me peace. Whenever I'd get insecure (which happened a lot), I'd quote the verses again and again. After a while, those fears no longer plagued me and I realized that four wonderful things had happened. First, I was sure I was saved. What a relief! I had confidence in my salvation. Second, truly, the fear of God is the fear that removes all others. Once I knew I was saved, I became much bolder and more confident around my peers. Third, I learned that I could control my thoughts and focus when I had to. Fourth, 42 years later, much to my pleasant surprise, I published an article entitled, "What Is the Unpardonable Sin?" for the *Christian Research Journal*.[2] I was honored to have the opportunity and see another way that the Lord used a grueling trial for my good and the good of others.

SUFFERING DEVELOPS GODLY CHARACTER: GETTING OFF THE GLORY TRAIN

Where jealousy and selfish ambition exist, there will be disorder and every vile practice.

JAMES 3:16

By my junior year in high school I was the 16-year-old coleader of a high school ministry on my campus. We had about 65 high school students meeting in my parents' house every Saturday night. The head of the ministry was 19, and I was second in charge. I taught Bible studies, and (I know this is bizarre, but it was during the Jesus movement) many of the students called me "pastor." Frankly, mentioning this is embarrassing.

I really did want to please the Lord, though this early success also fed a lust for human acclamation.

Soon, I set my ministry goal to being the pastor of a large mega-church. It was going to work like this: I would become the youth minister at a mega-church, then the associate pastor of a mega-church, then the senior pastor of a mega-church, and finally the senior pastor of an even bigger mega-church. Those were conscious thoughts I had all the time. I repeated them like a mantra in my mind (by the way, I never desired being on TV).

Well, as soon as I graduated from college, I started my Master's in Divinity (MDiv) program and became a high school youth minister in a church with about 10,000 people in regular attendance.

Check.

I was on my way. I felt I was God's man of power in the hour!

Sadly, however, the church's Christian education director didn't see in me the glory that was there. I felt he was holding me back from the recognition I deserved. He liked another youth guy better.

Although my position was secure, I became jealous over the lack of recognition. Let me say again that I really did want to please the Lord despite this worldly lust.

One day, the college pastor passed me as he was walking up the stairs to the church office and pronounced, "You're just trying to build your own little kingdom!"

I could have said a lot of things in response. I could have replied that he got me all wrong, that I *only* wanted to please the Lord (that would have been a lie). I could have said that I knew I had those lusts in my heart but that was something I was working on (that wasn't true either).

Instead, being very spiritual, I shot back, "So are you!"

I'd like to claim that at least I was being honest, but I'm not sure *he* was trying to build his own little kingdom. After all, I paid little attention to him because I was focused on *my* ministry.

Soon, my jealousy turned into bitterness. Then, I got tired. Very tired.

In fact, I got so tired that I would wake up, have breakfast, and take a nap. I'd wake up, have lunch, and take a nap. Then, I'd wake up, have dinner, and take a nap. And so on. I decided to self-diagnose my "extreme tiredness" and the first thing I stumbled upon was leukemia. Now I had another thing to worry about.

Finally, I went to the doctor. He ran some tests and told me that I was hypoglycemic. He told me to eat only protein and to start hard exercise daily. This did help, but only so much. Even so, I did want to please the Lord and was reading my Bible daily. I even apologized to a youth guy for being jealous of him.

But I was still a bitter, tired, and frustrated mess. I did so poorly in school that semester that I got put on academic probation even though I dropped all but one class.

Then one evening, I was in a pool playing Marco Polo with some high school students and, while underwater, I suddenly felt a sharp twang in my left shoulder. Two thoughts occurred simultaneously:

"I've just dislocated my shoulder" and "Be not like…a mule, without understanding" (Psalm 32:9). The latter thought struck me harder than the former.

When I surfaced, I announced, "I've just dislocated my shoulder!" One of the high school students said he knew how to reset my shoulder, so he stood on the deck while I was still in the water, and he started yanking my arm upward. We soon realized that he had no idea how to reset my shoulder. It got reset in the emergency room, and I was given a shoulder immobilizer, which meant that I couldn't run or do any other kind of meaningful exercise. So now, I had hypoglycemia, was constantly tired, was eating Big Macs without the buns, couldn't exercise, couldn't sleep comfortably, was jealous, was bitter, and felt like a ministry failure.

I was broken.

I knew I had been building my self-worth on my ministry success and now realized that this not only displeased the Lord, but He wasn't going to put up with it. I appreciated that. Really. I felt loved. A day or two later, I resigned from being a youth minister—effective immediately (sorry, CE director—I could have handled that better). I took stock of my life and repented for loving this world and for looking for glory from other humans.

I never again recited my "youth pastor of a mega-church, associate pastor of a mega-church, pastor of a mega-church…" mantra thingy.

I was humbled.

Not even remotely perfect, but different. I still had more to learn. You see, we humans can't simply stop lusting after the wrong things: We need to start lusting after the right things.

When I was finishing up my MDiv (my grades greatly improved), John Wimber hired me as an associate pastor of Calvary Chapel Yorba Linda, which became the flagship Vineyard Christian Fellowship. While I was on staff, church attendance went from an average of about 500 to 5,000 people. But I didn't say, "Check," this time. I had learned that I must not climb the ministerial-fame ladder, but instead, needed to please the Lord.

It turned out that I hadn't been the only one climbing that ladder. I began to dread communion services because it seemed that just about every time we had communion, someone would come up to me and confess the sin of hating me for getting the position he wanted. I'm not kidding. A senior pastor later half-kidded that when they brought me on staff, "half the guys in the church just about lost their salvation."

Thankfully, during my time there, the Lord began to reveal to me the glory that awaits us in heaven forever. What we all need is to learn to lust after God and His kingdom. After all, I know something about you and me (and by that, I mean everyone in the world): We are all full of lust. God created us all with strong desires. He could have created us with weak desires such that someone could say, "Hey look, your house is on fire," and we could turn around to look and slothfully reply, "So it is." But God created us with strong desires, and we are all going to lust after something. We're either going to lust after God and His kingdom or we're going to lust after people, possessions, positions, or pleasures. But no matter what, we are going to lust. The English New Testament translations sometimes do us a disservice here because they translate the Greek *epithumeo* as "lust" (e.g., 1 John 2:16 NIV, NASB) for wanting something sinful but as "desire" (e.g., Philippians 1:23 NIV, NASB) for craving something honorable.

As I began to fix my lusts/desires on God and His kingdom, the lust/desire for ministerial/worldly accomplishment greatly diminished. I can't say it completely went away because I'm not perfect at keeping my desire only for God and His kingdom—none of us are perfect and we live in a fallen world. Amazingly, I also found that sexual lust greatly diminished as I lusted for the glory that awaits us in heaven forever—what a blessing!

SUFFERING TEACHES AND PROTECTS US: AN UNPUBLISHED BOOK

Moses fled and became an exile in the land of Midian...
Now when forty years had passed, an angel appeared to him
in the wilderness of Mount Sinai, in a flame of fire in a bush.

ACTS 7:29-30

In 1994, I (Clay) started writing the book *Why Does God Allow Evil?* and submitted perhaps 25 proposals to publishers, all of which were turned down. In 2004, Biola University hired me to teach in their Master of Arts in Christian Apologetics program, and soon I started teaching the course Why God Allows Evil. It quickly became a required course in our program. Although I was frustrated about not publishing the book, I was pleased to be teaching the course to master's students.

Here's the good part. Many of our students were well-read, mid-career professionals—doctors, lawyers, engineers, professors, business owners, etc. Some would argue fervently with me. Thankfully, arguing with these students sharpened and polished my own arguments, and, as the years went by, it became increasingly easier to answer objections. Although it took a frustrating 23 years for my book to finally be published, I absolutely, positively thank God that He didn't allow me to publish it sooner. Let me emphasize that, *I thank God it wasn't published earlier!* If it had been printed sooner, I would have published a bunch of errors, other professors would have picked it apart, and it would not have been as persuasive as it is today. Thank You, Jesus, for not granting my prayers sooner!

SUFFERING PURIFIES US: FIRED WHILE SEEKING APPROVAL FROM OTHERS

For am I now seeking the approval of man, or of God? Or am I trying to please man? If I were still trying to please man, I would not be a servant of Christ.

GALATIANS 1:10

To date, it was the hardest six months of my (Jean's) adult life.

The head of a ministry team, "Sally,"[3] dropped me from leading a ministry I had played a large role in setting up. I popped my left shoulder out of joint and could barely use my arm. A nurse told me that lab tests showed all manner of sexually transmitted diseases (STDs) in my body and responded to my protest that it wasn't possible with a sarcastic, "It must have been the pool then." Sally's boss (the ministry leader) had previously asked me if I'd be willing to take Sally's position since she was relying on me for so much—I'd replied, "Only if she's okay with it." But now, he told me I shouldn't have done such a good job that she became suspicious. *Suspicious about what?* I wondered. I thought he was going to talk to her openly and see what Sally wanted. Meanwhile, Clay was having increasingly severe lower back pain.

Several emotional months later, I learned Sally had told blatant lies about me. I stopped trying to repair our relationship.

Less than two weeks later, Clay's doctor told him he had a tumor on his spine. My priorities shifted. I no longer obsessed over my damaged reputation. I cared only about my husband's life. But the lab diagnosed terminal cancer. While packing for the trip to Cedars-Sinai for his surgery, I further injured my shoulder, causing it to freeze.

Yes, it was a tough six months. Yet it was six months that revealed false beliefs I was holding to and made room for truth and growth in my life.

For example, I grew up being told I was responsible for other people's moods and actions. Going through this dark time revealed the folly of that belief.

My dad had told me that my mother hated me because he told her I was smarter than her. My mother told me I'd ruined her life and that I'd made a sibling suicidal by being better at school. So when the ministry leader told me I'd done too good a job, it added to the tremendous guilt I already carried over hurting people by causing jealousy. A good friend agreed with the ministry leader, saying I ran too far ahead of people and made them feel bad. But Clay responded to him, "Should I ask [famous author's name] to stop publishing books because it makes *me* feel bad?"

That made sense to me. I called my sibling. It turned out that my mother had lied about me being the source of my sibling's depression to hide her own culpability. It took time, but I learned that the burden of guilt I'd carried over my mom's jealousy wasn't my burden. It was hers.

God also used Sally to teach me that one of the reasons He tells us not to seek human approval is that doing so makes you easy to manipulate. Manipulative people neither like nor respect people pleasers. They see them as an easy means to their ends.

I saw my own complicity too. Before things went awry, I'd overheard Sally talking about a lie she told someone, and I said nothing. People pleasers have difficulty obeying Jesus' command, "If your brother sins, rebuke him, and if he repents, forgive him" (Luke 17:3). I also realized that willingly taking the blame for someone else's mistakes is dishonest. And I learned that believing the best of people doesn't mean ignoring evidence showing someone is acting sinfully.[4]

I discovered that I can survive slander and false accusations. The opinions of others do not change reality. Also, people who loved me cared about my feelings and didn't quickly reject me based on one person's accusations. Now, the opinions I care most about are those of thoughtful, mature Christians, and they are unlikely to accept accusations at face value but will weigh them along with other evidence.

I found out that I need not defend myself to be vindicated. Though defense seemed to be a just and winnable course of action, it could have damaged the ministry and the faith of younger Christians. Defending my reputation at the cost of damaging another's growing faith would have been losing. Encouraged by two wise friends, I decided not to defend myself other than to those involved. That has shown itself to be the right choice—the winning choice in the only race that counts.

I took comfort in Jesus' assurance to those who've been maligned: "Have no fear of them, for nothing is covered that will not be revealed, or hidden that will not be known" (Matthew 10:26). No lie can survive forever.

After Clay's surgery, we broke ties with the ministry. His doctor successfully removed the tumor, which was a treatable cancer. New lab work for me showed no STDs. Physical therapy and cortisone shots repaired my shoulder.

During this trial, I questioned why the God of truth was letting others believe lies about me. In reality, He did so to stop me from believing lies.

SUFFERING DEVELOPS GODLY CHARACTER: THE LORD DIDN'T MAKE ME A PASTOR—HE MADE ME A PROFESSOR

In all your ways acknowledge him, and he
will make straight your paths.

PROVERBS 3:6

When I (Clay) eventually left the Vineyard to start a church, I started a home Bible study and took a job as an underwriter in a major insurance company to support us. I was disappointed that I wasn't a full-time pastor. But I needed the self-discipline developed by working in the insurance industry. I learned about corporate seminars and navigating cocktail parties. I acquired the ability to quickly develop rapport with strangers. I learned to be more detail oriented (important when you're an underwriter) and to be nicer and more patient. I discovered what not to do, not only from my own mistakes, but from watching others crash and burn.

The Lord never again made me a pastor, but it turned out that He did something better (for me anyway). When I was in seminary, I didn't want to be a professor. I didn't want to teach on the same subjects again and again. But, oddly enough, the Lord made me a professor, and it turned out I much prefer teaching the same courses multiple times as opposed to developing a new sermon every week. I liked the sense of mastery that teaching a topic repeatedly brings. I loved teaching the class Apologetics Research and Writing every semester for 16 years. In addition, I loved teaching the course In Defense of the Resurrection, and I especially loved teaching Why God Allows Evil. And I often speak in churches and at conferences. The Lord knew what was best for me.

SUFFERING WELL ENCOURAGES OTHERS: LOSING MY CAREER

As we share abundantly in Christ's sufferings, so through Christ we share abundantly in comfort too. If we are afflicted, it is for your comfort and salvation; and if we are comforted, it is for your comfort, which you experience when you patiently endure the same sufferings that we suffer.

2 CORINTHIANS 1:5-6

When I (Clay) first started at Biola University, I "asterisked" the doctrinal statement on a small point of doctrine and wrote on the doctrinal statement next to the asterisk something to the effect that Biola's position on this issue might be 100 percent correct but I wasn't completely convinced. Thankfully, I was teaching unrelated subjects, so they let me teach in Talbot School of Theology's Master of Arts in Christian Apologetics program.[5] After 15 years of teaching, I was told that Biola was requiring every professor to sign Biola's doctrinal statement without reservation. They gave me a year to make up my mind, but I was still not able to sign it without reservation, so my contract was not renewed. Now, let me be clear, Biola acted honorably in the way they handled my situation. I do not fault Biola for anything—they were kind to me and acted fairly.

But I also had to keep a clear conscience, and that meant I was soon unemployed. This was a scary time for us. Were we going to need to sell our house and move into a smaller place? Would we need to move to where there would be a lower cost of living? Would we need to live off our retirement (we thought we were a little young to start burning through that)? Were we going to need to drastically cut back our lifestyle? What was I going to do for ministry? On top of this, there was the sadness of losing a career I loved, the loss of companionship with other faculty members, the loss of relationship with students, and the loss of health insurance. In short, losing my position at Talbot was a significant financial and emotional loss to both of us.

But we watched in awe as our Lord took care of us. His provision is amazing.

First, several people told us they would support us in our ministry, and they have. We formed a non-profit called Live for Eternity to help them do that. (As you've already seen in this book, encouraging people to live for eternity is much of what our lives are about.) Second, Jean was able to get Social Security and Medicare because she turned 65 exactly 30 days prior to my last day of employment with Talbot. I didn't yet qualify for Medicare and had to sign up for COBRA, which cost us around $700 a month. But then, much to our amazement, because of the COVID pandemic, the government decided to pay for my COBRA. In fact, the government stopped paying for COBRA the same month that I became eligible for Medicare. When it came to what I was going to do for ministry, COVID lockdowns allowed me to do dozens of podcasts, publish numerous articles, and we both wrote many blogs. Once travel restrictions subsided, I started speaking all over the United States again.

But most importantly, I was a man of integrity and that was a witness to thousands of people. One former student wrote the following to me in response to hearing why I was leaving Talbot:

> Dr. Clay, I just heard the news and am praying for you, fervently. You don't know this, but I was offered a job last month...that would've doubled my previous salary, if only I could affirm and promote their mission of LGBTQ. I wish I could say it was an easy decision, but I'd been out of work for over a year. I turned it down, only for them to up my benefit perks. Ultimately, I said no, but I wrestled with whether or not I should've taken it and tried (somehow) to not compromise my own beliefs. With that said, hearing why you left Biola not only encouraged me in my decision, but inspired me to stand my ground on all future offers. Thank you for being a beacon of light...

I'm thankful to say that many others from all over the United States and Canada who heard about my situation wrote me similar things. Sadly, several also wrote to me saying that they had been faced with a similar situation but didn't handle it as well.

I know the angels saw Jean and me. But most importantly, the Father saw us. We were willing to honor Him and keep a clear conscience even over a relatively small point of doctrine.

Losing my job was tough for us, but God delivered us.

SUFFERING WELL ENCOURAGES OTHERS AND IS A MEANS OF WITNESSING: AFIB AND CANCER (AGAIN)

Blessed be the…God of all comfort, who comforts us in all our affliction, so that we may be able to comfort those who are in any affliction, with the comfort with which we ourselves are comforted by God.

2 CORINTHIANS 1:3-4

"You should go to the emergency room now." A friend who is an emergency room doctor at a distant hospital spoke those words over my (Clay's) cell phone calmly and matter-of-factly. Jean had used her smart watch to measure my heart rate, and we texted him the results. My resting pulse bounced around 150-160 beats per minute. Although they did an EKG test right away, when I entered our community hospital, the ER waiting room was jammed and it took eight hours to finally get a room. I had atrial fibrillation (Afib), which causes an irregular and very fast heart rate. Once I was in the room, they started giving me drugs to slow my heart rate, but nothing worked. After a couple of hours, a woman performed an ultrasound and found a mass on my liver. The doctors referred me to my general practitioner to see what the mass was.

A subsequent PET scan revealed that I had metastasized cancer in my liver, lungs, and bones. Meanwhile, I had a periodontal surgery that didn't go well, and I'm now missing a molar (at least it doesn't show).

Honestly, I thought I'd be dead in less than a year. But now, medications are controlling my Afib, and here I am writing this two years later in no pain. My chief oncologist—the director of orthopedic oncology at Cedars-Sinai who surgically removed the same type of cancer from me 23 years ago—told us at one year in, I might not be in any pain for "three, five, seven, even ten years," but then he added, "or it could be six months." The six-months estimation didn't surprise us because we know that metastasized cancer is unpredictable. Since that diagnosis, I have endured many outpatient procedures like Y-90s, cryoablations, radio frequency ablations, and so on. We call it "Whack-A-Mole." As a particular lesion becomes threatening, they whack it.

As you can imagine, this can be stressful. But stress and suffering sooner or later force true Christians to act on those Scriptures that seem out of reach. We wrote "sooner or later" because when suffering strikes, we humans first resort to old coping mechanisms like denial, drink, drugs, or distraction (such as nonstop entertainment). But as suffering continues, there comes a point where the true Christian realizes that old coping mechanisms fail, and we need to start doing what Scripture says to receive long-term relief. For example, 1 Peter 1:13 says, "Preparing your minds for action, and being sober-minded, set your hope fully on the grace that will be brought to you at the revelation of Jesus Christ."[6] Focusing on eternity puts earthly problems into proper perspective. Still, we have never known a Christian who could obey that verse who hasn't suffered.

The long-term suffering we now endure forces us to regularly meditate on and *do* what Scripture commands. Remembering these passages helps us thank God for what He is doing in our lives: making us more like Christ. Although we know for a fact that Christianity is objectively true, nothing gives us *subjective* confidence in the truth of Christianity more than seeing suffering develop godly character in our lives.[7] So we can rejoice that our sufferings are conforming us into the image of God. A.W. Tozer is right: "It is doubtful whether God can bless a man greatly until He has hurt him deeply."[8] As Solomon puts it, "Blows and wounds scrub away evil, and beatings purge the inmost being" (Proverbs 20:30 NIV). Remembering how past sufferings helped us encourages us that God will use our present suffering to accomplish similar blessings.

Spurgeon says,

> Health is set before us as if it were the great thing to be desired above all other things. It is so? I would venture to say that the greatest blessing that God can give to any of us is health, *with the exception of sickness*. Sickness has frequently been of more use to the saints of God than health has. If some men, that I know of, could only be favoured with a month of rheumatism, it would, by God's grace, mellow them marvelously.[9]

I can recount many ways that this present suffering has blessed us. But one thing has really surprised me—how much God has used this! As we have asked for prayer on social media and expressed that Jean and I continue to honor God, many people have told me how I have encouraged them.

Here are some actual social media responses[10]:

- "Every update you share provides deep and powerful instruction to us for the battle in which we share. Thank you for the blessing of your remarkable testimony!"
- "Thank you for these encouraging updates, Dr. Jones. You're training us to face suffering in our own lives thru your approach. Thank you."
- "Professor, to see such a resilience, such a perseverance. The way you cling to God encourages us!!! With your testimony, with your endurance and with your faith!!! Thank you for touching my life in such a way!!"
- "This may be encouraging if you're going through a hard time (or ever have, or ever will). I firmly believe that we all need to be reading about those who have suffered more than

> we have and yet have remained steadfast in their faith and witness. Clay Jones has done just that, and now in these years of his own suffering, he is drawing from the perseverance and faithfulness of those whose stories he has read."

So, if you, dear Christian, are going through difficult times, share that with others who can pray for you and encourage you, and be encouraged as they see you honor God while you endure significant suffering.

In Philippians 4:5, Paul says, "Let all men know your forbearance. The Lord is at hand" (RSV).[11] Many translations differ on the Greek word for "forbearance." Some use "gentleness" (NIV), others "reasonableness" (ESV), but we prefer "forbearance" (RSV) as it sums up both. We are patiently hanging in there because Jesus is with us! Jean and I are persevering under trial. We continue to honor God through our suffering and are seeing that this encourages others to honor God when they suffer.

Also, I've become a much bolder witness. I've shared the truth of the resurrection of Jesus with many people, such as my gardener. Once he asked, "How are you, Mr. Clay?" I replied, "I'm well! I just found out that I have stage four cancer, but I'm a Christian and Jesus really was raised from the dead, so I know I have eternal life." And I've shared with many, many medical personnel—MRI techs, RNs, PAs, residents, and many MDs. One resident at Cedars-Sinai asked me how I was doing, and I said, "I'm doing well, thank you." He replied, "Can I ask why?" I said, "Because I'm a Christian and we have extrabiblical evidence that some of the first disciples gave their lives because they said they saw Jesus raised from the dead."[12] I then pointed out that although it's true that people die for what they think is true that later turns out to be false, no one dies for what they *know* is false. I said more than this, and to some I've said much more than this. I probably spoke for 15 minutes with one young woman who was training to be an MRI tech. It turned out she was already a Christian, but she didn't know there was evidence for the truth of Christianity. It made her happy.

In the next chapter, we'll expand on how God uses truth 3 in every Christian's life.

5

TRUTH 3, PART 2: GOD WILL WORK SUFFERING OUT FOR OUR GOOD

In chapter 4, we (Clay and Jean) gave specific examples of how our Father has worked good things through suffering in our lives. Unless you're relatively new to abiding in God's Word, you too have seen God use suffering to work wonderful things in your life. We look forward to hearing about your triumphs in the ages to come![1] If you haven't been abiding in God's Word, trust Him; and as suffering comes into your life, you will be able to see how God uses it for your good here on earth. In this chapter, we will expand on what Scripture says about how our Father uses suffering to work good things in all our lives both here on earth and throughout eternity.

SEEING OTHERS SUFFER WELL ENCOURAGES US: ABRAHAM'S BIRDS OF PREY

God uses even the mundane things in our lives to bless others. One of the greatest blessings in honoring God through suffering is how it encourages others. As we ourselves have openly shared what we are going through, how we trust God, and how God helps us, many Christians have replied that they have been blessed and encouraged.

The Bible's stories of those who suffered well can encourage us. For example, Genesis 15:1 tells of an encounter between the Lord and the childless Abram (later called Abraham): "The word of the Lord came to Abram in a vision: 'Fear not, Abram, I am your shield; your reward shall be very great.'" But in verse 3, Abram complained, "Behold, you have given me no offspring." In response, the Lord "brought him outside and said, 'Look toward heaven, and number the stars, if you are able to number them.' Then he said to him, 'So shall your offspring be.' And he believed the Lord, and he counted it to him as righteousness" (verses 5-6). It's because of this that Abraham is called the father of our faith.[2] The Lord then tells Abram in verses 9-10, "'Bring me a heifer three years old, a female goat three years old, a ram three years old, a turtledove, and a young pigeon.' And he brought him all these, cut them in half, and laid each half over against the other. But he did not cut the birds in half."

This is one of the most important events in the whole of Scripture.

But in verse 11, we read something odd: "And when birds of prey came down on the carcasses, Abram drove them away." Here the father of our faith was honoring God in this spiritually foundational moment but had to keep driving away the birds of prey. Those pesky birds! The Lord could have kept the birds away. After all, the Lord ordered the birds to feed Elijah (1 Kings 17:4-6). But the Lord let the birds do what carnivorous birds do: try to feast on fresh meat. I (Clay) am thankful that the bird of prey story was included in Scripture because it shows that even in our most spiritual moments, hardship happens.

Recently, this story encouraged me. I had an outpatient procedure where they burned two lesions on my pelvis via radio frequency ablation. It went well—no nerve damage (thank You, Lord!). But when they wheeled me out, the nurse, and later, the anesthesiologist told my wife that I would have trouble urinating. I felt fine, and after they discharged me, I went to the bathroom to pee. It. Hurt. Like. Crazy. Agony! The next day during a follow-up call, a nurse asked me the pain level I experienced, and I answered, "8.5. And there was a lot of blood." It turned out, when they inserted the catheter, they nicked the inside of my urethra. When going to the bathroom for the next few days, I thought to myself, "And Abraham had to keep chasing away the birds of prey." That encouraged me. Stuff happens. Thankfully it only took about 24 hours for *most* of the pain to stop, and in a couple of days I was fine.

Exactly one week after that procedure, the leader of our church small group unexpectedly asked, in front of the group, about my catheter event (I had told him earlier and he thought it was funny, and I kind of did too). So I shared with the group about the pain and the blood. Then, I explained my consideration of Abram's story. Surprisingly, when I mentioned my reflecting about the painful urination I endured and my thoughts of the birds of prey, some of the women teared up. One woman, whose husband had recently had a successful open-heart surgery, told the group she was encouraged because it made her realize that hardship is to be expected, even when you're trying to please the Lord.

SUFFERING WELL DEVELOPS GODLY CHARACTER THAT BRINGS HOPE

Twenty-three years ago, when a doctor told me that I (Clay) likely had terminal cancer, 2 Corinthians 1:8-9 were my favorite verses: "We do not want you to be unaware, brothers, of the affliction we experienced in Asia. For we were so utterly burdened beyond our strength that we despaired of life itself. Indeed, we felt that we had received the sentence of death. But that was to make us rely not on ourselves but on God who raises the dead."[3] After a while Jean and I got to the point where we thought and said, "Well, we're just going to have to trust the Lord." Although Clay's cancer 23 years ago turned out to be treatable, this latest occurrence wasn't caught early enough. We are again in a state of, "Well, we're going to have to trust the Lord," and that is exactly what our Lord wants. The Lord uses suffering to develop godly character so that we can become more like Him and can accomplish much for His kingdom.

Paul writes, in Romans 5:2-4, "Through him we have also obtained access by faith into this grace in which we stand, and we rejoice in hope of the *glory* of God. Not only that, but we rejoice in our *sufferings*, knowing that suffering produces endurance, and endurance produces character, and character produces hope." Notice that the word *glory* is found near the word *suffering* again. So how does suffering produce hope? Suffering produces endurance. Endurance is the ability to "hang in there" even while things are tough. Babies don't have endurance. If they aren't fed, changed, hugged, given a toy, or whatever, they cry or scream. We've all seen woefully indulged older children who still throw tantrums when they don't get their way. We also know older adults who were so coddled as children that they expect instant gratification and to be catered to. But the Father will not put up with that. He graciously allows suffering in our lives. We may whine or scream, but for our good He won't give in.

All the fruits of the Spirit require endurance—the ability to hang in there, to persevere, to put up with adverse circumstances. You can't love people if you can't put up with their faults. You can't have joy or peace if little things annoy you. And so on. Endurance fosters character. As we see God fulfill His promise to build character, our hope increases.

Hope for what? Hope that we will share in the glory of God that is manifest in our lives as we obtain His character through suffering.

As Clay mentioned in his unpardonable sin trial, when it was over, he realized that he was more like Jesus. Although we know that Christianity is objectively true because of the evidence for the resurrection of Jesus, nothing makes us realize that Christianity is subjectively true more than seeing suffering work godly character in our lives. Suffering has made us more like God and that is evidence that

Christianity is true—we really are going to live forever and inherit His kingdom (more about that later).[4]

James 1:2-4 reads, "Count it all joy, my brothers, when you meet trials of various kinds, for you know that the testing of your faith produces *steadfastness*. And *let* steadfastness have its full effect, that you may be perfect and complete, lacking in nothing." Steadfastness is the same thing as endurance—the ability to persist under trial. Thus, if we "let" it, in time, our suffering makes us "perfect and complete." Then, in verse 12, James writes, "Blessed is the man who remains steadfast under trial, for when he has stood the test he will receive the crown of life, which God has promised to those who love him." There it is again. Remain "steadfast under trial" is another way of saying continue to honor God through suffering. When you do, you will receive the "crown of life." God is making us glorious through suffering.

Earlier we explained how much Jesus endured and how that demonstrates God's love for us. Hebrews 12:3-4 tells us that we should "Consider him who endured from sinners such hostility against himself, so that you may not grow weary or fainthearted. In your struggle against sin you have not yet resisted to the point of shedding your blood." I (Clay) often remind myself that I'm not in a foul dungeon waiting to be tortured to death! Hebrews 12:5-7 reads,

> And have you forgotten the exhortation that addresses you as sons?
>
> "My son, do not regard lightly the discipline of the Lord,
> nor be weary when reproved by him.
> For the Lord disciplines the one he loves,
> and chastises every son whom he receives."
>
> It is for discipline that you have to endure. God is treating you as sons. For what son is there whom his father does not discipline?

Notice "It is for discipline that you have to endure" or, as the NIV puts it, "Endure hardship as discipline." When we are going through something hard, we should ask ourselves what our Father is seeking to teach us. Let us not be as passive as a mud puddle; let's examine why God has brought suffering into our lives. Hebrews 12:8-11 continues:

> If you are left without discipline, in which all have participated, then you are illegitimate children and not sons. Besides this, we have had earthly fathers who disciplined us and we respected them. Shall we not much more be subject to the Father of spirits and live? For they disciplined us for a short time as it seemed best to them, but he disciplines us for our good, that we may share his holiness. For the moment all discipline seems painful rather than pleasant, but later it yields the peaceful fruit of righteousness to those who have been trained by it.

At the beginning, our suffering may only feel painful, but later "it yields the peaceful fruit of righteousness." Our Father is making us like Jesus, and that's eternally praiseworthy.

SUFFERING TEACHES US NOT TO LOVE THIS PRESENT WORLD

Suffering helps us not love this present world. It helps us ignore the world's song and, if we submit to it, forces us to focus on eternal life in Jesus. Thus, the Lord allows us to be surrounded by, sometimes swamped by, suffering and death to keep us from loving this present world.

First John 2:15-17 commands:

> Do not love the world or the things in the world. If anyone loves the world, the love of the Father is not in him. For

> all that is in the world—the desires of the flesh and the desires of the eyes and pride of life—is not from the Father but is from the world. And the world is passing away along with its desires, but whoever does the will of God abides forever.

Occasionally I handle pesticides, and I've learned the difference between notices labeled "Caution," "Warning," or "Danger." *Caution* means "it *may* cause minor or moderate injury." *Warning* means "it *can* cause death or serious injury." *Danger* means "it *will* cause death or serious injury." One pesticide I saw at Home Depot warned that it was fatal if inhaled and caused irreversible eye and skin damage. Well, I don't value anything in my yard enough to use that pesticide!

So, DANGER: Do not love the world.

But this isn't easy, right? It's natural, all too natural, for us to seek the shiny baubles, the shimmering knick-knacks, and the sparkling playthings of this world. And that's exactly where suffering comes in. The Lord uses suffering to teach us not to love this world but rather to love Him and the kingdom to come. Once we realize the importance of not loving the world—but instead understand the plan of being transformed into God's likeness and being prepared to inherit His kingdom—all the sickness, suffering, and death in this world start to make sense. He's trying to teach and train us to reign with Jesus now and forever.

SUFFERING HONORABLY TEACHES US TO REIGN IN OUR BRAIN

In chapter 4, we read 2 Corinthians 10:5: "We destroy arguments and every lofty opinion raised against the knowledge of God, and take every thought captive to obey Christ." Taking our thoughts captive requires two things we will address now: remembering God's past deliverances and focusing on eternity. (We'll develop this further in chapter 7.)

We Must Remember God's Past Deliverances

It isn't enough to mouth that God has always worked hardship out for our good. We need to remember our past deliverances, and the best way to remember them is to record them—that is, write them down. Listing them makes it easy to recall specific examples of how God has used suffering for our good.

The Lord regularly exhorted the Israelites to "remember" His past deliverances. For example, in Exodus 13:3 Moses said to the people, "*Remember* this day in which you came out from Egypt, out of the house of slavery, for by a strong hand the LORD brought you out from this place." As they prepared to enter the promised land, the Lord told them, "Only be careful, and watch yourselves closely so that you *do not forget the things your eyes have seen or let them fade from your heart* as long as you live. *Teach them* to your children and to their children after them" (Deuteronomy 4:9 NIV).

Later, the Lord said to them in Deuteronomy 7:17-19,

> You may say to yourselves, "These nations are stronger than we are. How can we drive them out?" But do not be afraid of them; *remember well what the LORD your God did* to Pharaoh and to all Egypt. You saw with your own eyes the great trials, the signs and wonders, the mighty hand and outstretched arm, with which the LORD your God brought you out. The LORD your God will do the same to all the peoples you now fear (NIV).[5]

"Remember." "Do not forget." Do not let God's prior deliverances "fade from your heart." "Teach them."

Contemplating God's past deliverances enables you to rein in your brain. It assures your heart that God will deliver you again.

Philippians 4:8 reads, "Finally, brothers, whatever is true, whatever is honorable, whatever is just, whatever is pure, whatever is lovely, whatever is commendable, if there is any excellence, if there is anything worthy of praise, think about these things." God's past deliverances are all these things, so we should keep them in mind.

WHAT TO DO NOW: CREATE A TRUTH JOURNAL

To help us remember God's past deliverances, we both keep what we call truth journals. Clay keeps his in a Word document. He changes the font color of anything related to eternity to purple, the color of royalty. Jean has a tab in the back of her daily planner labeled "TRUTHS." Our journals have pages with these titles:

- **Truths**—Personalized statements based on Scripture: "The Lord is all-powerful, and He loves us."
- **Remembrances**—Blessings God has given us and prayers He has answered in providential ways. We've recorded the deliverances mentioned in chapter 4 and many more.
- **Scripture**—Passages that bring us peace: "I have said these things to you, that in me you may have peace. In the world you will have tribulation. But take heart; I have overcome the world" (John 16:33).
- **Prayers**—A list of prayer requests and answers, plus passages that we pray, such as Philippians 4:4-7. Jean also includes a prayer based on Psalm 71.

SUFFERING PREPARES FOR US AN ETERNAL WEIGHT OF GLORY

Some years ago, our friend Janet, wife and mother of two young children, endured a series of difficult and painful surgeries due to metastasized breast cancer. On one particular day after brain surgery, she sent out an email with the wryly titled subject line, "Lobotomy Results," in which she described her doctor drilling into her skull. Despite her pain, she emailed friends regularly with encouragement. At her memorial service, her husband described how moments before she died, she stood up in her bed with arms raised as if she were seeing someone coming to get her.

From childhood, I (Jean) have thought in pictures and symbols more than in words.[6] Not long after Janet discarded her cancer-ridden body and entered God's presence, Clay and I drove to San Diego. I stared out the window at the ocean and prayed for Janet and her family. An image appeared in my mind's eye of Christ taking Janet by the hand and lifting her out of a shadowy line of people onto the bright, raised platform on which He stood. He proudly presented Janet before the Father and heavenly beings. The short wisps of hair chemo had left her became a thick mane of blonde tresses cascading down her back. A golden crown encrusted with emeralds shimmered upon her head.

Before ascending, her earthly body was frail and weak. Now her body was straight and strong, the muscles of her bare arms full and rounded. Light radiated from her. The shapeless tunic she had worn before Christ raised her transformed into a glittering gown woven of fine bronze filaments, a symbol of strength. It gathered at the top of her sturdy shoulders and draped in folds beneath her collarbone before cascading to her feet. A thin bronze belt with a bejeweled clasp encircled her waist.

Her face showed amazement and overwhelming joy.

Below the platform stretched a long line of dim people, ghostly representations of those whose bodies hadn't died yet, including myself. We looked like a murky river of souls weaving among pale mountains, indistinct as if caught in dusk.

Only a few near the platform seemed to notice it. A teenage girl in a frilly dress looked at Janet and asked why *she* was so lucky. A man explained to her that it was because Janet had been a great witness for God: She had gone through great suffering but remained faithful. The girl replied, "But that's not fair! I haven't gotten to suffer much, so how will I get a chance to be adorned like that?"[7]

I smiled, thinking how quickly we forget, and how backwards we have it here on earth. If only we on earth could glimpse eternity's perspective. The Scriptures provide us previews, but do we have eyes to scc?

This being said, we don't think anyone in heaven will wish they had suffered more on earth. As with every man I know, I (Clay) admire the accomplishment of becoming a Navy SEAL. But I do not wish that when I was younger, I had gone through SEAL training—too much suffering! But the larger point remains, those who suffer greatly in this life will be awesomely rewarded in the next. Here, everyone wants to avoid suffering, and we consider those who don't as unfortunate. Yet in heaven, those who go through the hardest things with faith will be considered the most honored and blessed. And that honored blessedness will last forever.

How Suffering Is Connected to Glory

First Peter 1:3-9 connects glory with suffering. In verses 3-5, Peter writes,

> Praise be to the God and Father of our Lord Jesus Christ! In his great mercy he has given us new birth into a living hope through the resurrection of Jesus Christ from the dead, and into *an inheritance that can never perish, spoil or fade.*

> This inheritance is kept in heaven for you, who through faith are shielded by God's power until the coming of the salvation that is ready to be revealed in the last time (NIV).

We love these verses! We've been promised "an inheritance that can never perish, spoil or fade." Our inheritance cannot die, it cannot rot or decay, it cannot wilt or tarnish. No one can steal it. Our inheritance will now and forever be "brand new"; it won't get scratched or dented. This is true because it's kept in heaven for us. And it's no small thing.

Peter continues in verse 6, "In all this you greatly rejoice, though now for a little while you may have had to *suffer* grief in all kinds of trials" (NIV). There it is: Presently, we "suffer grief in all kinds of trials." Then, Peter tells us why we suffer in verse 7: "These have come so that the proven genuineness of your faith—of greater worth than gold, which perishes even though refined by fire—may result in praise, *glory* and honor when Jesus Christ is revealed." Notice that "glory" is again linked to our honorably enduring suffering. So as we honor God through suffering, it proves our faith to be real, and we will receive "praise, glory and honor" when Jesus is revealed.

In verses 8-9, Peter concludes, "Though you have not seen him, you love him; and even though you do not see him now, you believe in him and are filled with an inexpressible and glorious joy, for you are receiving the end result of your faith, the salvation of your souls." So even though we suffer, we are joyous because of the glorious future that awaits us! People have asked us how it's possible to be joyous and grieve at the same time. As we noted in the introduction, at a wedding, the parents of the bride and groom often experience grief and joy at the same time.

Second Corinthians 3:7 is another amazing glory passage. Paul reminds us that when Moses spoke with the Lord and then returned to talk with the people of Israel, "the Israelites could not gaze at Moses' face because of its glory."[8] Then Paul asks in verse 8, "Will not the ministry of the Spirit have even more glory?" "Indeed," writes Paul, the old covenant was glorious but "what once had glory has come to have no glory at all, because of the glory that surpasses it. For if what was being brought to an end came with glory, much more will what is permanent have glory" (verses 10-11). Much. More. Glorious.

Paul continues, and we all, who "contemplate the Lord's glory, are being transformed into his image with ever-increasing glory, which comes from the Lord, who is the Spirit" (verse 18 NIV).

Only a few verses later, in 2 Corinthians 4:7, Paul writes, "But we have this treasure in earthen vessels, so that the surpassing greatness of the power will be of God and not from ourselves" (NASB1995). Notice that the "treasure" is *in* the earthen vessel or jar. Earthen jars were, as Murray J. Harris puts it, "regarded as fragile and as expendable because they were cheap and often unattractive. So the paradox Paul is expressing is that although the container is relatively worthless...the contents are priceless."[9] But for those spiritually dead to God, the treasure *is* the earthen jar because there isn't anything inside of value until a person is born again.

Paul continues:

> We are afflicted in every way, but not crushed; perplexed, but not despairing; persecuted, but not forsaken; struck down, but not destroyed; always carrying about in the body the dying of Jesus, so that the life of Jesus also may be manifested in our body. For we who live are constantly being delivered over to death for Jesus' sake, so that the life of Jesus also may be manifested in our mortal flesh (verses 8-11 NASB1995).

When the earthen jar is damaged, the treasure inside it is revealed to us, to the world, and to heavenly beings in the presence of Almighty God.

An Eternal Weight of Glory Comes

Next comes what we consider the most important, most encouraging verses regarding our present suffering and the eternal glory that awaits us, 2 Corinthians 4:16-18:

> So we do not lose heart. Though our outer self is wasting away, our inner self is being renewed day by day. For this light momentary affliction is preparing for us an eternal weight of glory beyond all comparison, as we look not to the things that are seen but to the things that are unseen. For the things that are seen are transient, but the things that are unseen are eternal.

Notice that Paul says that our affliction, our suffering, is "preparing for us an eternal weight of glory."[10] It doesn't say that *we are being prepared* for an eternal weight of glory (although that too is true), but that our suffering here *is preparing for us* an eternal weight of glory. As Harris puts it, "In the divine economy, affliction actually generates glory." He continues, glory "is not presented as a reward for suffering, as if suffering of itself were meritorious." Rather, glory "is the God-ordained outcome" of suffering.[11] It's simple: As we honor our Lord through the hardships of this life, then we will enjoy an "eternal weight of glory."

We are called to be faithful in anything the Lord asks us to do. This faithfulness may include everything from getting out of bed to go to work so that we can feed our family or care for the disabled to honoring God through severe pain or physical persecution. These are types of suffering, and the Lord expects us to be faithful in whatever He allows to come our way. And we can be faithful in our suffering by keeping our eyes on eternity.

In 2 Corinthians 5:1-2, we read, "For we know that if the tent that is our earthly home is destroyed, we have a building from God, a house not made with hands, eternal in the heavens. For in this tent we groan, longing to put on our heavenly dwelling."[12] Indeed! Life in our earthly tents is tough and "while we are still in this tent, we groan, being burdened," but we await the time when "what is mortal" will be "swallowed up by life" (verse 4). Verses 6-8 read, "So we are always of good courage. We know that while we are at home in the body we are away from the Lord, for we walk by faith, not by sight. Yes, we are of good courage, and we would rather be away from the body and at home with the Lord." Did you get that, dear Christian? Paul basically says that we're better off when our bodies die because then we will be swallowed up by life! So "we make it our aim to please him. For we must all appear before the judgment seat of Christ, so that each one may receive what is due for what he has done in the body, whether good or evil" (verses 9-10). So now, here, we endure "light momentary affliction," but Paul encourages us that as we honor Jesus we will be richly rewarded throughout eternity.

Therefore, even in immense suffering, we remind each other, "The Lord always works every hard thing out for our good." "Every hard thing out for our good." "He always has and always will."

6

TRUTH 4: MANY HAVE HONORED GOD THROUGH HARSHER SUFFERING THAN WE HAVE

Jean: "Many have had it harder than we have it but still honored God."

Clay: "Yes, I'm not in a stinking, stifling dungeon waiting to be slowly roasted to death."[1]

In chapter 1, I (Jean) shared that I prayed, "Everyone else can have children; why can't I?" Without realizing it, I had felt entitled to be a mom. A sense of entitlement is often the foundation upon which anger at God rests. Immediately, I remembered that most single women have neither child nor spouse—in other words, if they desired both, then they had it harder than me. This cured entitlement. Entitlement's double-dose antidote was (1) grasping that God owes me nothing, and (2) remembering that many have suffered more while remaining faithful. Few things help more during suffering than realizing others have suffered worse yet still honored God through it. In fact, whenever things are tough—and they have been often lately—we remind ourselves that others have suffered more than we have while honoring God through it. This bolsters us.

Honoring God through suffering involves two major things. First, rejoicing in our suffering, which we've already examined. Second, taking care neither to grumble about our suffering nor to complain about God's goodness when we are suffering. For example, when David suffered God's severe chastisement, he wrote, "I said, 'I will guard my ways, that I may not sin with my tongue; I will guard my mouth with a muzzle, so long as the wicked are in my presence'" (Psalm 39:1). David resolved not to complain in the presence of unbelievers lest he sin by giving them reason to fault God. Instead, he spoke to the Lord, asking for guidance, mercy, and relief.

Remember Job's response after the Lord allowed Job's children and servants to be killed and all his livestock to be killed or stolen. "Job arose and tore his robe and shaved his head and fell on the ground and worshiped. And he said…'The LORD gave, and the LORD has taken away; blessed be the name of the LORD'" (Job 1:20-21). The next verse says, "In all this Job did not sin or charge God with wrong" (verse 22). Job didn't accuse God of wronging him.

The worship leader and psalmist Asaph responded similarly. He had lived according to God's commands, but he lacked the riches, good health, and honor that the wicked had. He wondered whether keeping God's commands had gotten him anything. Envy embittered his heart, his "feet had almost stumbled," and his "steps had nearly slipped" (Psalm 73:2). In his heart Asaph wondered:

> This is what the wicked are like—
>   always free of care, they go on amassing wealth.
> Surely in vain I have kept my heart pure
>   and have washed my hands in innocence.
> All day long I have been afflicted,
>   and every morning brings new punishments
>   (verses 12-14 NIV).

But in the next verse Asaph writes, "If I had spoken out like that, I would have betrayed your children" (verse 15 NIV). Asaph refused to betray the spiritually young by questioning God's goodness in front of them. Rather, amid his confusion, he sought answers from God, prayerfully laying out ways it seemed God was permitting injustice.[2]

When Asaph sought answers from the Lord, he saw that God's final justice awaits eternity (verse 17). Meanwhile, God was guiding and helping him (verses 23-24). He recognized sinful envy had skewed his perceptions. Glimpsing the glory to come enabled him to release that for which he had been striving: "Whom have I in heaven but you? And there is nothing on earth that I desire besides you. My flesh and my heart may fail, but God is the strength of my heart and my portion forever" (verses 25-26).

There is a lesson here for us. Asaph didn't publicly accuse God of unfairness, which would have disheartened young believers and emboldened unbelievers. Instead, he took his confusion to God: "But when I thought how to understand this, it seemed to me a wearisome task, until I went into the sanctuary of God; then I discerned their end" (verses 16-17). In doing so, Asaph remembered that final judgment comes. He then viewed good and evil, riches and poverty through an eternal perspective. That is necessary if we are to understand why God allows evil and suffering. In verse 24, he writes, "You guide me with your counsel, and afterward you will receive me to glory." Notice how the eternal perspective caused Asaph to extol God's goodness and abandon his earlier belief that he was being treated unfairly. An eternal perspective enables us to honor God through suffering and so humiliate Satan and his minions.

Asaph's and Job's responses to suffering taught them similar lessons—lessons that resulted in worship.[3] God revealed to them that He had been with them even when they didn't feel His presence (Psalm 73:23-24; Job 38:2). They discovered God was far greater than they imagined (Psalm 73:26; Job 42:2-5). Each of them more fully grasped that God owes people nothing (Psalm 73:25; Job 41:11) and that God had a wonderful eternal future for them (Psalm 73:24; Job 19:25-27).

Like them, we conquer and are victors (both forms of the Greek word *nike*) when we continue to honor God through hardship without complaining against Him.[4] Remembering those like Job who honored God through greater suffering than we endure helps us do likewise.

HOW REMEMBERING OTHERS STRENGTHENS US

In January of 2004, I (Clay) was lying in a hospital bed six days after surgeons removed my tailbone, the bone above that one, and half of the bone above that. I didn't know at that time whether the cancer they removed was fatal or treatable. After six days in the hospital, the hospital staff told me they were going to remove my catheter to see if I could urinate. They told me I might not be able to and that I might have to remain catheterized for a few months or maybe for life.

After the catheter was removed and I was contemplating the future ahead of me, I thought of Joni Eareckson Tada. Joni has always been a hero to me. Joni (pronounced *Johnny*) has been a quadriplegic since 1967, when she dove headfirst into shallow water in Chesapeake Bay and broke her neck. She was 17 years old at the time. So lying in the hospital, knowing I might be catheterized for life, wondering whether my cancer was fatal, and knowing that if they had to take much more bone from my spine I'd be a paraplegic, I thought of Joni. And I thought, *Wow, whatever I'm going through isn't as bad as what Joni has gone through and look at how she honored God through it! If Joni can do it, I can do it.* And I told the Lord that I would honor Him no matter what.

At that moment I felt famous. Although my suffering was much less than that of Kayla Mueller, Corrie ten Boom, and Richard Wurmbrand, it was still scary to me. Yet I also felt loved by God.

By the way, when they pulled the catheter, I was able to pee (inquiring minds want to know).

Even though Jean and I were alone in that hospital room, I felt famous because I knew the Father saw me, I knew angels saw me, and I knew that all humans would sooner or later know that I had honored God through suffering. I thought, *If Joni could honor God through decades of quadriplegia, then I can honor God through this.*

Joni Eareckson Tada

It is inspiring to know that Joni was helped by someone else too. The following is from an interview of Joni on *Larry King Live*:

> The thing that helped me most was getting my attention off myself and helping other quadriplegics who were more functionally limited than I was. I'll never forget when I was in occupational therapy, they were teaching me how to write with a pencil between my teeth, and I kept spitting it out on the floor. I mean, that's for disabled people, I'm not going to do that. But my occupational therapist would wipe it off with alcohol, stick it back in my mouth. And finally they wheeled into occupational therapy this ventilator-dependent quadriplegic named Tom. And my therapist went up to him and said, now, Tom, you can't use your hands, giving him the same spiel she gave me, but you're going to have to learn how to do things with your mouth. Here, take this pencil and let's see you practice writing the alphabet. And in my heart of hearts, I was saying, come on, Tom, spit it out, spit out the pen. But when I watched him laboriously, meticulously begin to write A, B, C, I felt so ashamed of myself. And I realized that there were other people with more pressing challenges and greater needs than me. And I wanted to help them.[5]

Notice that what helped Joni was seeing someone who had it worse than her.

Nick Vujicic

Some years ago at our church, we heard Nick Vujicic speak (pronounced Voy-a-chich). It was shocking when we first saw Nick because he was born with no arms or legs. But Nick knows Jesus, he's eloquent, and no one can dismiss him with the snarky statement, "Yeah, but what do you know about suffering?" We can barely imagine how difficult his life must be.

In his autobiography, *Life Without Limits: Inspiration for a Ridiculously Good Life*, Nick writes,

> My mum often read to me as a child, and one of my favorite books was *The God I Love*. I was about six years old when she first read it to me. At that time I didn't know of any other person born without arms and legs. I had no role models who looked like me and had the same challenges. This book, which I still think of often, inspired me and helped build the foundation for an attitude of gratitude because it was written by Joni Eareckson Tada.[6]

Wow, right? Nick writes: "For my part, I came to see that as great as my challenges were, many people had heavier burdens than mine."[7] It might strike you as odd, dear reader, that Nick would say there were people who had it harder than him but, even though he doesn't have legs, he has feet and is able to move around. He can even use his toes as fingers. In short, he's more mobile on his own than Joni.

Martyrs

One of the strongest examples in my mind of those who've had it harder than me are the many people who've been slowly tortured to death because of their faith in Jesus. What follows is difficult to read, but we need to be aware of what other Christians have suffered. Consider that if you, dear reader, were tortured to death for Christ, would you feel okay if everyone refused to hear about it? Understanding what others have suffered helps put our problems into perspective. W.E.H. Lecky in his *History of European Morals* sums up the Roman torture of Christians:

> Those hateful games, which made the spectacle of human suffering and death the delight of all classes, had spread their brutalizing influence wherever the Roman name was known, had rendered millions absolutely indifferent to the sight of human suffering, had produced in many, in the very centre of an advanced civilization, a relish and a passion for torture, a rapture and an exultation in watching the spasms of extreme agony...The most horrible recorded instances of torture were usually inflicted, either by the populace, or in their presence, in the arena. We read of Christians bound in chains of red-hot iron, while the stench of their half-consumed flesh rose in a suffocating cloud to heaven; of others who were torn to the very bone by shells, or hooks of iron; of holy virgins given over to the lust of gladiator or to the mercies of the pander; of two hundred and twenty-seven converts sent on one occasion to the mines, each with the sinews of one leg severed by a red-hot iron, and with an eye scooped from its socket; of fires so slow that the victims writhed for hours in their agonies; of bodies torn limb from limb, or sprinkled with burning lead; or mingled salt and vinegar poured over the flesh that was bleeding from the rack; of tortures prolonged and varied through entire days. For the love of their Divine Master, for the cause they believed to be true, men, and even weak girls, endured these things without flinching, when one word would have freed them from their sufferings.[8]

Indeed, "one word would have freed them from their sufferings." For example, Polycarp was a disciple of the apostle John who became bishop of Smyrna in AD 115. Thirty to 40 years later, a Roman governor warned Polycarp he would burn him at the stake unless he gave a public, token acknowledgement to Caesar as Lord. Polycarp refused to call Caesar "Lord" and was burned at the stake.[9]

Remembering these martyrs helped us when Clay's contract wasn't renewed at Talbot (discussed in more detail in chapter 4). Although Clay lost a ministry opportunity he loved, the companionship of other faculty members, relationship with students, his salary, and our health insurance, he often considered that all this loss—which was significant—was still a far cry from being imprisoned and tortured to death.

Remembering others' hardships puts our problems into perspective. In 2004, when I (Clay) had bone cancer the first time, my tailbone throbbed and lying down flat on my back on the MRI machine's hard surface was agonizing. I had to lie there, not moving, for about 55 minutes at a time. While I was lying there, I comforted myself by thinking of those who had been tortured. I thought, *Many Christians have had a lot more pain intentionally inflicted upon them than I am going through right now. If they could honor God through that, then I can honor God through this.* These thoughts didn't stop the pain, but they encouraged me.

Faithfully enduring suffering honors God because as we continue to maintain our witness and refuse to complain that God is unfair, we prove ourselves worthy inheritors of His kingdom.

SUFFERING WELL IS EVIDENCE OF FAITH

Caregivers often suffer while helping another (perhaps a spouse, child, friend, or new acquaintance). Regarding the mid-third-century pandemic in Carthage, Cyprian, the bishop of Carthage, describes those afflicted as having "bowels, relaxed into a constant flux" and "continual vomiting; that the eyes are on fire with the injected blood." He says that "in some cases the feet or some parts of the limbs are taken off by the contagion of diseased putrefaction." This resulted in "either the gait is enfeebled, or the hearing is obstructed, or the sight darkened." But then he adds that this "is profitable as a proof of faith. What a grandeur of spirit it is to struggle with all the powers of an unshaken mind against so many onsets of devastation and death!"[10] Cyprian says this is a "proof of faith" because this "horrible and deadly" pestilence was "necessary" for examining the human race, to see whether the healthy cared for the sick, "whether relations affectionately love their kindred; whether masters pity their languishing servants; whether physicians do not forsake the beseeching patients." He continues that if "this mortality conferred nothing else" it benefits Christians because "as we learn not to fear death" we "prepare for the crown."[11] So, dear Christian caregiver, if we care for the sick or injured, we are not alone. We can honor God through it.

In 2 Thessalonians 1:4-5, Paul writes, "Among God's churches we boast about your perseverance and faith in all the persecutions and trials you are enduring. All this is evidence that God's judgment is right, and as a result you will be counted worthy of the kingdom of God, for which you are suffering" (NIV). Notice that our honoring God through suffering is "evidence" to heavenly and earthly creatures that God's judgment about us is "right"![12]

Some might ask, "But if God knows our hearts, why does He need to prove our faith?" But the Lord isn't proving our faith to Himself. The Lord is proving our faith to everyone who sees us honorably endure suffering in this present age—Christians and non-Christians. And at the judgment, when all our deeds are revealed, He will reveal our proven faith to every sentient being. Everyone in the history of creation—humans, angels, and every other kind of celestial being—will get to see that you and we honored God through trial, thus proving that God's judgment about us is right and so we are "worthy of the kingdom of God"!

Enduring suffering is evidence that God's judgment is right. Believers' patient endurance of suffering proves their faith. The repentant are to "demonstrate their repentance by their deeds" (Acts 26:20 NIV), which include being faithful under trial. Thus, Jesus says that it is those who "endure to the end" who will be saved (Mark 13:13).

CONSIDER SUFFERING A PRIVILEGE

Paul writes in Philippians 1:29, "It has been granted to you that for the sake of Christ you should not only believe in him but also suffer for his sake." God has "granted" to us to "suffer for his sake." That is remarkable. About this, D.A. Carson writes,

> Their call to suffer on behalf of the gospel has been *granted* to them: it is a gracious gift from God! Not only have they enjoyed the privilege of coming to faith, they currently enjoy the privilege of suffering for Christ—"not only to believe on him," Paul writes, "but also to suffer for him."
>
> That is not the way we normally think of suffering, not even the suffering of persecution. But that is what Paul says. *If their salvation has been secured by the suffering of another on their behalf, their discipleship is to be demonstrated in their own suffering on his behalf.* Surely this should not be surprising. In what sense could it be said of us that we follow Jesus Christ, if there is no cross-bearing in our life?[13]

Sometimes Christians mistakenly think that suffering for Christ's sake refers only to persecution from sharing the gospel. But no. Anytime we honor God through suffering, we are testifying to the world that our faith in a loving God stands. Therefore, believers can count all affliction as being for Jesus' sake. Remember too that sometimes we suffer because Satan persecutes us. For instance, Satan afflicted Job to show Job wasn't as righteous as he appeared. But as Job honored God through suffering, he proved Satan's accusations false and God's judgments true (Job 1–2).[14]

We are surrounded by a great cloud of witnesses who suffered immensely while looking forward to their glorification, just as Jesus looked forward to His. Hebrews 11, "the hall of faith" chapter, lists such witnesses. We'll quote the last few verses here:

> Women received back their dead by resurrection. Some were tortured, refusing to accept release, so that they might rise again to a better life. Others suffered mocking and flogging, and even chains and imprisonment. They were stoned, they were sawn in two,[15] they were killed with the sword. They went about in skins of sheep and goats, destitute, afflicted, mistreated—of whom the world was not worthy—wandering about in deserts and mountains, and in dens and caves of the earth. And all these, though commended through their faith, did not receive what was promised, since God had provided something better for us, that apart from us they should not be made perfect (Hebrews 11:35-40).

They were mocked, imprisoned, stoned, sawn in two, and endured other heinous treatment because they maintained their witness to the end, and they died not having received "what was promised."

Only a few verses later, Hebrews 12:3-4 encourages those who were suffering increasing persecution in Rome: "Consider him who endured from sinners such hostility against himself, so that you may not grow weary or fainthearted. In your struggle against sin you have not yet resisted to the point of shedding your blood." As we discussed in the chapter on how God loves us, crucifixion was what the Romans considered to be the most excruciating way to execute someone, and here, the author of Hebrews is telling us to intentionally remember, ponder, reflect upon Jesus' suffering so that we don't grow "weary or fainthearted" when we suffer in our "struggle against sin." Jesus suffered and honored God through it. Like Jesus, we can honor God through suffering, and at our judgment we will be commended for our faithfulness and ushered into eternal joy.

So if you feel like you're going through more suffering than many other Christians, take heart. As someone has put it:

> When God wants to drill a man
> And thrill a man
> And skill a man
> When God wants to mold a man
> To play the noblest part
> When He yearns with all His heart
> To create so great and bold a man
> That all the world shall be amazed,
> Watch His methods, watch His ways!
> How He ruthlessly perfects
> Whom He royally elects!
> How He hammers him and hurts him
> And with mighty blows converts him
> Into shapes and forms of clay
> Which only God can understand!
> How He bends but never breaks
> When his good He undertakes
> How He uses whom He chooses
> And with mighty power infuses him
> With every act induces him

To try His splendor out!
God knows what He's about.[16]

When we're going through suffering, it's easy to feel as if our life is harder than others'. But if we do, consider the words of A.W. Tozer: "If God has singled you out to be a special object of His grace you may expect Him to honor you with stricter discipline and greater suffering than less favored ones are called upon to endure. If God sets out to make you an unusual Christian He is not likely to be as gentle as He is usually pictured by popular teachers."[17] Too often, Christian leaders have misrepresented Christianity as being something easy. But Jesus says, "If anyone would come after me, let him deny himself and take up his cross daily and follow me" (Luke 9:23). Tozer continues, "A sculptor does not use a manicure set to reduce the rude, unshapely marble to a thing of beauty. The saw, the hammer and the chisel are cruel tools, but without them the rough stone must remain forever formless and unbeautiful."[18] Similarly, C.S. Lewis writes in *The Screwtape Letters*, that "He [the Lord] relies on troughs [suffering] even more than on the peaks; some of his special favourites have gone through longer and deeper troughs than anyone else."[19] God uses suffering to give us godly character, and those who have godly character are capable of being faithful here.

So, dear Christian, when you suffer, consider it a privilege. Honor God through it, looking to those who've suffered more than you yet still honored God. You will defeat Satan.

7

TRUTH 5: WE DON'T KNOW WHAT TOMORROW WILL BRING

Clay: "We don't know what tomorrow will bring."

Jean: "No, we don't know what tomorrow will bring."

Twenty-three years ago, I (Jean) prayed that Clay's MRI would show that whatever was causing Clay's lower back pain wouldn't be serious. It wasn't hard to hope for that, because the orthopedic surgeon said the chances of it being serious were slim.[1]

But the MRI showed a tumor.

I prayed it would be benign. Again, it wasn't hard to hope for that, because the oncologist said the chances of it being malignant were extremely small.

But the lab diagnosed a rare form of bone cancer.

The oncologist said hospital labs sometimes misdiagnose rare cancers because they see them so seldom, so he wanted to see the slides himself before he decided how to proceed.

When I hung up the phone, I searched the Internet for information on the diagnosis. The first link I found confirmed it was rare, alright. And 100 percent fatal within two years. Panic hit me like ice water, and my heart pounded in my ears. I closed my computer and walked away.

I prayed the lab was wrong. But it was hard to hope for that. I didn't tell Clay what I'd seen.

Over the days that followed, worries whirled through my mind. Would he live? If not, how would I manage without him? If so, would he be disabled? Even if the lab were wrong, would surgery and recovery cost him the new job he was to start the next week? How would we manage financially?

I thought I needed to pray until I found peace in every possible scenario. But my prayers jumbled into each other as I prayed over one anxious "what-if" to the point of reaching peace, only to have a "what-if-not" start the whirling again. For example, fear that Clay might die would grip me. So I prayed, committing myself to trusting God over living alone, selling the house, moving, and so on until I calmed down. But then a new anxiety would sneak in: *What if he lives but loses his new job?* So I'd start a new prayer, committing to trust God that He'd take care of us financially and would guide Clay to a new job. But then—wham!—another thought assailed me: *What if he lives but is paralyzed and cannot find work?* Then I started praying over those circumstances, committing to trust God with finding a new job, upgrading the house, supporting Clay, etc. But praying until I found peace over that possible future left me vulnerable again to *What if he dies?*

I needed to pray a different way—a way that stopped trying to address all the possible tomorrows, a way that found hope bigger than human assurances.

I made two changes. First, I applied Jesus' words about worries to my daily prayers: "Do not be anxious about tomorrow, for tomorrow will be anxious for itself. Sufficient for the day is its own trouble" (Matthew 6:34). I stopped trying to come to peace with every possible future in that day's prayers. God hadn't called me to have today the strength I'd need for tomorrow. Most of the futures wouldn't happen anyway. Instead of praying over possible futures, each day

I prayed for the grace to meet that day's challenges with faith, and I committed to faithfulness no matter what, because I remembered my purpose: to proclaim God with my life and words.

The second change I made was to write out a prayer based on Psalm 71. I had done so in difficult times before and found it brought peace. It shows us how to pray with increasing and continual hope when trouble strikes.

So I wrote a new prayer based on Psalm 71. Enemies were out for the psalmist's life. I had enemies too: cancer and spiritual enemies. So where the psalmist wrote about human enemies, I wrote about cancer. He asked for God's help based on God's righteousness; I prayed based on God's power to heal and comfort. The psalmist recalled God's past deliverances; I wrote about God's past help in my own life. He honestly described his fears and desires; I did the same, substituting my own. I wrote out the psalm's theme: "But I will hope continually and will praise you yet more and more" (Psalm 71:14). The psalmist looked forward to how he could serve God; I did the same, remembering my purpose. He looked further forward to eternity and rejoiced in how eternity would make all things right; my prayer did too.

How different this prayer was than the anxious prayers I'd been praying. It filled me with hope. It asked for help today, then it looked to the parts of the future that are certain: ministry until God calls us to Him, a judgment in which all will be made right, and a glorious resurrection. Writing out this prayer meant that any time anxiety seized me, I could pray this prayer. It instantly calmed me and refocused my eyes.[2]

In time, we saw parts of the answer to the good God intended through Clay's cancer. The first laboratory's diagnosis of Clay having a fatal, fast-growing cancer was mistaken. It was a slower-growing cancer caught early enough to be treatable. He lost his teaching contract for only one class, but soon after, Biola University hired him part time to oversee online courses from home while he recovered. That led to a full-time teaching position at Biola the following semester. His experience gave weight and authority to his class on why God allows evil.

The first cancer journey was part of God's purpose and plan to bring people to know Him.

WE REALLY DON'T KNOW WHAT TOMORROW WILL BRING

The first time we spoke to one of Clay's interventional radiologists during our present cancer journey, he pointed to a couple of lesions on Clay's pelvis and told us that he would do a cryoablation on them. *Okay*, we thought, *that works.* But then he pointed to four other places and said he couldn't do a cryoablation on them because they were too close to nerves. We didn't say so, but we left his office disappointed because we thought that those lesions couldn't be treated. But after he performed the cryoablations, he told us that he would do radio frequency ablations on the other lesions. *What?* He did so, and there were no negative side effects. We wish he had told us during our first meeting that there were other treatments for the four lesions, but apparently it didn't occur to him. Or the Lord simply wanted us to have one more thing to trust Him over. Frankly, we think it's both.

During this cancer journey, we've often felt trapped, much like Israel did with the Red Sea in front of them and Pharaoh's army behind them. Clay's cardiologist delayed treating his heart with a cardiac ablation until the cancer was in remission. But it took five months and multiple biopsies to correctly diagnose the cancer as one for which there was no treatment to put it into remission. His new medical oncologist at Cedars-Sinai wanted to enter Clay into a clinical trial that showed promise, but the trial's testing showed that Clay's heart had no longer met the minimum strength requirements to qualify for the clinical trial. Of course, we were sad that a potential cure wasn't available, but we also realized that these are clinical *trials*—that is, experiments—that might not succeed. We didn't want Clay to endure medications with significant side effects that would ultimately prove a failure. So here was another opportunity to trust God.

Cedars-Sinai began treating the most threatening lesions. However, by that time, Clay had been in chronic Afib too long for a cardiac ablation to succeed. Still, we're thankful that medications strengthened his heart to the point that, as of this writing, his heart is just barely below the minimum strength required to be in a clinical trial. In the meantime, we're thankful that Clay bypassed the side effects of trials that proved unsuccessful. Just as Israel went through the Red Sea when God parted the waters, so we go through any doors the Lord opens.

One series of events especially illustrates how we don't know what tomorrow will bring, so we should trust God when it seems there's no way forward. Since Clay's cancer doesn't respond to regular radiation, one of his oncologists requested proton beam radiation. Only two places in Southern California do that. One of them wouldn't take our insurance, and the other told us that they weren't willing to do it until Clay had pain. Clay's primary oncologist thought waiting until the cancer reaches nerves was a mistake. That made sense to us, but again we felt trapped. Nonetheless, we prayed and thanked God and just kept trusting Him.

Five months later, a new spine oncologist joined our team. He was the director of the program that specializes in Clay's cancer at one of the most famous East Coast research hospitals. When we told him that we weren't able to get approval for proton beam therapy, his response was that it isn't the type of radiation Clay needs. Rather, Clay needs stereotactic radiation, and that requires only one to three applications and is performed only ten minutes from our house. Proton radiation would have been 75 minutes from our house, five days a week for eight weeks. Thank You, Jesus! Also, the new oncologist affirmed that he wouldn't order radiation unless Clay felt pain. For now, Clay's immune system is keeping the tumors from growing, so there is no need.

DON'T WORRY ABOUT TOMORROW

Every person, sooner or later, realizes that many of the things we humans worry about never happen. As Mark Twain put it, "I am an old man and have known a great many troubles, but most of them never happened."[3] Worrying about tomorrow wastes today. As Jesus says in Luke 12:22-23, "I tell you, do not worry about your life, what you will eat; or about your body, what you will wear. For life is more than food, and the body more than clothes" (NIV). It's easy to think, *But I need food, or I will die, and I need clothing, or I will freeze to death!*[4] But, as usual, Jesus emphasizes the relative unimportance of our bodily needs. For Jesus, everything, including sustenance and warmth, modesty, and so on, is relatively unimportant in comparison to right relationship to Him. This, of course, doesn't mean that food and clothing are of no importance, so Jesus says in verses 24-26, "Consider the ravens: They do not sow or reap, they have no storeroom or barn; yet God feeds them. And how much more valuable you are than birds! Who of you by worrying can add a single hour to your life? Since you cannot do this very little thing, why do you worry about the rest?" (NIV).

Recall, in Matthew 6:34, Jesus says, "Do not worry about tomorrow, for tomorrow will worry about itself. Each day has enough trouble of its own" (NIV). Indeed, worrying about the future doesn't help us add even an hour to our lives. Of course, planning for some future event may be exactly what we need to do today. But there's a big difference between planning for tomorrow and worrying about tomorrow!

DON'T LOOK AT THE WIND

One day, Jesus sent off the disciples in a boat while He dismissed the crowds and prayed alone. Late that night, as the disciples toiled against the wind and crashing waves, Jesus came to them, walking on the waves. They thought He was a ghost and cried out, but Jesus told them not to be afraid, for it was He. Peter said if it really was Jesus, then command him to walk on the water to Him. Jesus obliged and said, " 'Come.' So Peter got out of the boat and walked on the water and came to Jesus" (Matthew 14:29). But "when he saw the wind, he was afraid, and beginning to sink he cried out, 'Lord, save me' " (verse 30). Then, "Jesus immediately reached out his hand and took hold of him, saying to him, 'O you of little faith, why did you doubt?' " (verse 31). All of us know why Peter doubted and began to sink: He looked at the wind instead of Jesus.

"Looking at the wind" is what Clay and I (Jean) call worrying about what *might* happen. Since we found out Clay has stage-four cancer, plenty of temptations to look at the wind have come. For example, one evening we heard a woman talk about losing her husband, and I thought, *What if I can't manage alone?* Potential problems tossed like waves in my head. A tear trickled down my cheek, and Clay asked gently, "Are you looking at the wind?" "A bit," I replied, and then we recited the truths we *know* about the future.

Of course, there are what we call "windy days"—days when we have a doctor visit, Clay has a procedure, or we get news from tests. We've found that unless the news is great, it forces us to look at the wind at least for a bit as we process the news. But then we remind each other we don't know what tomorrow will bring, so don't look at the wind.

While we generally look only to the day's problems, former Navy SEAL Chad Williams explains how he looked at an even smaller chunk of problems when facing the challenges of SEAL training. He writes:

> I had learned to narrow my perspective to the task at hand. It was too challenging to think, I've gotta make it through this day. It was better to think, I've gotta make it through this one evolution. Then I would do the same with the next evolution. I wouldn't think any further ahead than that.

> And I never thought about the remainder of Hell Week. If I had done that—and I suspect this is what happened to those who were dropping out—I easily would have become overwhelmed by what lay ahead.[5]

And that's what we need to learn: to focus on the task at hand and not to consume ourselves with tomorrow's *potential* problems.

WHAT TO DO NOW: TAKE EVERY THOUGHT CAPTIVE

We must "take every thought captive to obey Christ" (2 Corinthians 10:5). We must remind ourselves not to worry about tomorrow. It takes discipline! We must simply not let our minds go there. Instead, Paul tells us in Philippians 4:6: "Do not be anxious about anything, but in every situation, by prayer and petition, with thanksgiving, present your requests to God" (NIV).

Indeed, as we explained in chapter 3, we often pray Philippians 4:4-6, beginning with, "Rejoice in the Lord always; again I will say, rejoice," and continuing by rejoicing over the good God has worked through hard things in the past. By the time we get to "The Lord is at hand" (verse 5) and start thanking Him for being right there with us, we're ready to present our requests with thanksgiving. So instead of worrying, ask God for help and thank Him for the hardships we endure.

But what about in the middle of the night when thoughts are hard to control? Sometimes I (Clay) find waking up difficult because I can't control my dreams. As I'm waking up, I'll realize that my dreams were worrisome. So, what do I do? I start singing Christian songs. I started doing this when I was in college because I often woke up in the dark and I'm *not* a morning person (I often joke, "I'd get up to see the sunrise if it didn't come so early in the morning"). So getting up in the dark, I'd sing. And I'd recite aloud encouraging verses like Psalm 118:24: "This is the day that the Lord has made; let us rejoice and be glad in it."

Sometimes I'll think a dire thought about the future. I'll push it out of my mind, but find it still brings me down. So I'll figure out what about it is making me sad ("Why are you cast down, O my soul?"), bring it up to the Lord, remind myself of the seven truths, and tell Him I'm trusting Him over that issue. Then, I go back to focusing on Jesus and eternity.

Are possible problems weighing heavily on you? Are tomorrow's anxieties spoiling today? Then get your mind off what might never happen and fix your eyes on Jesus. Don't let the prospect of a negative possible future ruin your today. Not only do we not know what tomorrow may bring, God will work everything out for our eternal good. And that leads us to our next point: Instead of worrying about tomorrow, focus on Jesus and the race set before us.

8

TRUTH 6: FOCUS ON JESUS AND THE RACE SET BEFORE US

Clay: "Hi, racer!"

Jean: "Hi, racer!"

Clay: "Hi, high adventurer!"

Jean: "Hi, high adventurer!"

While I (Jean) waited for doctors to perform a second biopsy on Clay's liver during his current cancer journey, I sat on a wooden bench under a shady tree, listening to birds sing. I pulled out my tablet, opened a Bible in the Kindle app, and turned to Hebrews 12. When I finished reading, I slipped my tablet back into my purse and stood. As I walked along the dirt paths that meandered among trees and manicured lawns, I pondered verses 1-2:

> Since we are surrounded by so great a cloud of witnesses, let us also lay aside every weight, and sin which clings so closely, and let us run with endurance the race that is set before us, looking to Jesus, the founder and perfecter of our faith, who for the joy that was set before him endured the cross, despising the shame, and is seated at the right hand of the throne of God.

Only three months prior, our general practitioner had told us Clay almost certainly had stage-four cancer, and no oncologist would treat cancer that advanced. Thinking Clay wasn't likely to live out the year, I considered two things. The first was that this great cloud of witnesses might include millions of saints who now resided in heaven. Many of the women who are there had been widowed because often, married women outlive their husbands. The fact that I wasn't alone in what I faced comforted me. Although I doubted that the saints in heaven were watching, just in case any were, I said, "Hi, all you saints! Thanks for cheering us on. You completed the race faithfully, and I can do it too with God's help."

The second thing I considered was that Jesus showed us how to face death, whether our own or a loved one's. He endured the cross and despised its shame. How? By focusing on the joy that was set before Him—the joy of bringing a multitude of believers into eternal life with Him. When we faced painful procedures such as biopsies, we could endure it. If Clay or I, at any time, became incontinent, we could despise the shame. We could do both by focusing on the joy that is set before us: an end to pain and sickness, a glorious resurrected body, and eternal life in the new heavens and earth together with loved ones and the God who did all this for us.

"It is appointed for man to die once," Hebrews 9:27 reads. Barring the Lord's return, you and I and everyone we know will die. Everyone is going to go through this—because death is the passageway to heaven.

Suffering reminds us of this truth and thereby helps us not love this present world. John writes, "Do not love the world or anything in the world. If anyone loves the world, love for the Father is not in them. For everything in the world—the lust of the flesh, the lust of the eyes, and the pride of life—comes not from the Father but from the world. The world and its desires pass away, but whoever does the will of God lives forever" (1 John 2:15-17 NIV). John commands us to not love this present world. Suffering is the best remedy to loving this world. Pain focuses our eyes on the eternity to come.

PINK ELEPHANTS

There's an old brainteaser, "Think about whatever you want, but for the next two minutes don't think about pink elephants."[1] Most everyone knows that the way you keep from thinking about pink elephants is to think about blue elephants. In other words, we need to distract ourselves.

The ability to keep certain thoughts in our consciousness to the exclusion of other thoughts is fundamental to self-control. The Lord commanded Israel to control their thoughts. The main trouble with texting while driving is that it distracts us from keeping our thoughts on what our car is doing in relation to what the cars or pedestrians or animals or whatever around us are doing. Many people are maimed or killed because they did not pay attention to their driving. Similarly, many Christians live sad, depressed lives because they don't remember that God loves them and is working all things together for their good (Romans 8:28).

Just as Israel was told to keep certain thoughts in their heads to the exclusion of other thoughts, we Christians are told that there are certain thoughts that we must keep in our heads. Namely, we're to keep our thoughts on Jesus and on eternity.

Looking to Jesus

In the previous chapter, we talked about Peter walking on water but beginning to sink when he looked at the wind instead of Jesus. We likened looking at potential problems to looking at the wind. We shouldn't focus on potential problems that might never happen. But the only way not to look at our potential problems is to look at something better. Hebrews 12:1 encourages us: "Since we are surrounded by such a great cloud of witnesses…let us run with perseverance the race marked out for us" (NIV). The witnesses are the faithful heroes listed in Hebrews 11. Their lives bore witness to their faith and are examples for us. They not only faced the loss of loved ones—all but Enoch faced their own deaths. By "witnesses" it doesn't mean they are literally watching us here on earth (often, that's a good thing), but that they were witnesses for God during their earthly lives and now know that we are running a race similar to theirs and may be cheering us on. Certainly angels, our Father, and our Lord Jesus Christ are watching us, ready to aid. And at the judgment, our faith, which was tested here on earth, will be revealed and rewarded (1 Corinthians 4:5).

We remind ourselves that what we are going through is "the race marked out for us." Yes, it took an unexpected turn, but it's what is marked out for us, so we must run it with perseverance. That is why Jean and I remind ourselves of this by sometimes greeting each other, "Hi, racer." We also greet each other with "Hi, high adventurer" because we are on an adventure—a high adventure—even though both of us would prefer to stay in the Shire.[2]

We love that we are surrounded by a great cloud of witnesses who have suffered immensely but who were looking forward to their glorification as Jesus looked forward to His!

Earlier we quoted Hebrews 12:1-2, which shows the application of the faith chapter to our lives. It tells us that as we run our race, we must look "to Jesus, the founder and perfecter of our faith, who for the joy that was set before him endured the cross, despising the shame, and is seated at the right hand of the throne of God" (verse 2). In other words, Jesus kept His eyes on the prize. By pursuing the joy that would come at the end of His race, Jesus "endured the cross, despising the shame." In chapter 2, we mentioned the shame of Roman crucifixion and how the victims hung dying, naked, and had to publicly urinate and defecate to relieve themselves. And Jesus is God! Honoring God by enduring what the world called shameful, in reality, brought Him glory. Jesus is our example. Just as He looked to the joy to come and was thereby able to endure pain and despise earthly shame, so can we. Glory awaits.

Paul writes similarly in 1 Corinthians 9:24-25: "Do you not know that in a race all the runners run, but only one receives the prize? So run that you may obtain it. Every athlete exercises self-control in all things. They do it to receive a perishable wreath, but we an imperishable."

Eternal joy and glory await us at the end of our races too. Paul writes, "He will render to each one according to his works: to those who by patience in well-doing seek for glory and honor and immortality, he will give eternal life" (Romans 2:6-7). Later, in Romans 8:16-17, he writes, "The Spirit himself bears witness with our spirit that we are children of God, and if children, then heirs—heirs of God and fellow heirs with Christ, provided we suffer with him in order that we may also be glorified with him." That is why we too can persevere through pain and despise what we might normally consider the shameful aspects of suffering, such as losing hair to chemo or needing someone to clean us when we cannot control our bowels. Joy comes and glory awaits.

I (Clay) interviewed several Navy SEALs, and what stood out to me the most was that during their often-torturous training, they kept their eyes on the prize. They could "drop" at any time and "ring the bell," but the thought of attaining the SEAL trident pin and becoming a SEAL kept them going. (Their second biggest driver was the embarrassment of failure.) So, when Jean and I are having a really hard time, we'll quote to ourselves, and often to each other, Hebrews 12:1-2 (yes, we've both memorized it). We may follow it with, "We're coming to be with You, Jesus. We're coming to be with You."[3] Many times when I have awakened in the middle of the night, I've told the Lord, "I'm coming to be with You, Jesus. I'm coming to be with

You." Knowing that if we endure hardship honorably, we too will be eternally exalted helps immensely.

Looking to Eternity

First Peter 1:13 tells us, "Preparing your minds for action, and being sober-minded, set your hope fully on the grace that will be brought to you at the revelation of Jesus Christ." That's not three commands; that's one command. We are to prepare our minds for action and be sober-minded so that we can set our "hope fully on the grace that will be brought to you at the revelation of Jesus Christ." So much for the mindset "Live in the moment." Our hope needs to be set on a future event—*The Future Event*—when we will receive grace at the revelation of Jesus! We will talk more about our future blessings in chapters 9 and 10.

Similarly, Colossians 3:1-4 is one of our favorite passages that we quote to each other regularly: "If then you have been raised with Christ, seek the things that are above, where Christ is, seated at the right hand of God. Set your minds on things that are above, not on things that are on earth. For you have died, and your life is hidden with Christ in God. When Christ who is your life appears, then you also will appear with him in glory." There it is again: God intends to glorify us. The Christian's life is hidden now but will be revealed in glory. People look at us now and may think that we are nothing. Nerds. Neurotics. Nincompoops. But we will be revealed in glory. Seek the things above! Set your mind on the things above, to the exclusion of earthly things. Of course, we don't do that automatically. We naturally set our minds on things here. But our Father wants—demands—that we set our minds on things above. As Murray Harris puts it, "Christians should be characterized by a fixation on invisible, eternal realities. Paradoxically, their eyes are riveted on what cannot be seen. The world of sense does not determine their outlook and action."[4] Learn to appreciate that suffering helps us—compels us—to focus on Jesus.

Therefore, dear Christian, decide to honor God through suffering so that when suffering comes and you honor God through it, you will receive "praise, glory and honor when Jesus Christ is revealed" (1 Peter 1:7 NIV).

And that brings us to Truth 7: We will forever enjoy a glorious eternity together.

9

TRUTH 7: WE WILL FOREVER ENJOY A GLORIOUS ETERNITY TOGETHER

Jean: "We're going to be together forever."

Clay: "Yes, we're going to enjoy each other forever and ever."

Cartoons like *Tom and Jerry* first introduced heaven to me (Jean). They showed spirits rising from bodies and traversing a golden escalator up to heaven's gate. The Sunday funnies depicted heaven's residents as wearing white tunics and bearing halos, harps, and wings while standing on fluffy white clouds chatting nonchalantly. Later, the *Adventures of Huckleberry Finn* told me that heaven is boring and filled with unpleasant people, with all the fun folks in the other place. Not surprisingly, I had fuzzy, inaccurate pictures of heaven floating in my mind.

So do most people.

In fact, many Christians have such an anemic view of heaven that they fear it will be dreadfully boring. Some fear that eternal rewards won't be rewarding. That's a problem because the New Testament encourages us to persevere through suffering and difficulties because God will reward us with eternal life. But if we don't think the rewards will be worthwhile, persevering will be just short of impossible.

In his books, *Why Does God Allow Evil?* and *Immortal*, Clay refers to Satan's propaganda regarding eternal life as "Extreme Makeover Metaphysical Edition."[1] Satan seeks to paint a picture of heaven so boring and unattractive that no one would want to go there, and few would persevere through hardships. For us to persevere in hardship, heaven must be more than simply "better than the other place."

In this chapter, we'll look at five facets of our glorious inheritance that await those belonging to Jesus. In the process, we'll blow aside some cloudy myths.

GLORIOUS INHERITANCE 1: OUR PERSONS

Myths about our eternal persons abound, including that we will be angels and will lose our senses of taste, smell, and touch. Let's dispel those first.

Myth: The Saved Become Angels When They Die

In Charles Dickens's book, *The Old Curiosity Shop*, a child says to Little Nell, "Why, they say...that you will be an angel, before the birds sing again."[2] In other words, Little Nell will die and become an angel before daybreak.

But Scripture doesn't teach that. The idea misunderstands Matthew 22:30, which reads, "For in the resurrection they neither marry nor are given in marriage, but are like angels in heaven." Jesus' point in this passage is that resurrected people are *like* angels in that they can't die. Because they can't die, they don't need to procreate. They aren't born of mommy and daddy angels. Instead, God created the angels before He created the earth (Job 38:4, 7).[3]

Myth: The Saved Can't Taste, Smell, or Touch

Many Christians fear that heaven will be less than what we have on earth. The movie *City of Angels* (1998) portrays it as such. In that movie, angel Seth (Nicholas Cage) has no sense of taste, touch, or smell. As the movie progresses, he falls in love with human Maggie (Meg Ryan) and gives up his angelic status ("falls") to become human so that he can have sex with Maggie, which he does. But the next morning, a truck kills Maggie as she is out riding her bike. Later, another angel asks Seth if it was worth giving up his immortal status to become human. He replies, "I would rather have had one breath of her hair, one kiss from her mouth, one touch of her hand, than eternity without it. One."[4] That's dumb: He'd give up eternity just for one chance to smell her hair? In other words, for Seth, eternal life was an everlasting bummer.

No verse in the Bible tells us that throughout eternity we won't be able to taste, touch, or smell, as depicted in *City of Angels*. Throughout eternity we are going to have glorified bodies like Jesus' post-resurrection body. He ate (Luke 24:42-43), and He could be hugged (John 20:17). Again, this misconception is Satan's work.

The Three Stages of Eternal Life

Part of the confusion about our persons has to do with how the Bible describes eternal life in three stages.

Stage 1 of Eternal Life: The Born-Again State

Once we are born again, we are in what we call the first stage of eternal life. This is the born-again state: God, "even when we were dead in our trespasses, made us alive together with Christ" (Ephesians 2:5). Most Christians think in terms of "Yes, I'm going to live forever" without fully appreciating that our living forever has already begun. We are *presently* eternal beings. This solves humankind's greatest need—we need to escape death and the judgment—and we have! We are, right now, living forever.

Timothy Keller relates a version of an often-told story that puts the Christian's death into its proper perspective:

> Donald Grey Barnhouse, who was a pastor at Tenth Presbyterian Church in Philadelphia for many years, lost his wife when his daughter was still a child. Dr. Barnhouse was trying to help his little girl, and himself, process the loss of his wife and her mother. Once when they were driving, a huge moving van passed them. As it passed, the shadow of the truck swept over the car. The minister had a thought. He said something like this, "Would you rather be run over by a truck, or by its shadow?" His daughter replied, "By the shadow of course. That can't hurt us at all." Dr. Barnhouse replied, "Right. If the truck doesn't hit you, but only its shadow, then you are fine. Well, it was only the shadow of death that went over your mother. She's actually alive—more alive than we are. And that's because two thousand years ago, the real truck of death hit Jesus. And because death crushed Jesus, and we believe in him, now the only thing that can come over us is the shadow of death, and the shadow of death is but my entrance into glory."[5]

In John 8:51, Jesus says, "Truly, truly, I say to you, if anyone keeps my word, he will never see death." As we mentioned in chapter 3, Jesus wasn't in denial; He knew we would die. But our entry into the intermediate state will be seamless. We'll only notice that things are better—much better—than they were.[6]

Stage 2 of Eternal Life: The Intermediate State

The second stage of eternal life begins when our physical bodies die and our souls go to be with God in the heavenly realm. Theology professor Alan Gomes writes, "The intermediate state, both for Christians and for unbelievers, is disembodied." Christians will have "direct and glorious communion with Christ and an immediate apprehension of God's presence—far more so than anything enjoyed in this life."[7]

As Jesus says to the thief crucified next to Him, "Truly, I say to you, *today* you will be with me in paradise" (Luke 23:43). *Paradise* is one of the Bible's names for the current state of heaven.[8] People sometimes call it *transitional heaven* or *present heaven*. In Revelation 6:9, John describes seeing humans in heaven like this: "I saw under the altar the souls of those who had been slain for the word of God and for the witness they had borne." And Paul writes, "While we are at home in the body we are away from the Lord...and we would rather be away from the body and at home with the Lord" (2 Corinthians 5:6, 8). In other words, to Paul the intermediate state was preferable to his spirit being in his still-living physical body. When humans are young and strong, this doesn't seem so desirable. But as our bodies age, this transition grows ever more attractive to us. Being a disembodied spirit won't be a problem for us because until the creation of the new heavens and earth, we won't need a body to interact with a physical world.

There will be no delay. In fact, your transition into the unseen realm will be so smooth, so seamless, so natural, that it may take you a while to realize that you've died. When Christians die, we will instantly transition "to the city of the living God, the heavenly Jerusalem, and to innumerable angels in festal gathering, and to the assembly of the firstborn who are enrolled in heaven, and to God, the judge of all, and to the spirits of the righteous made perfect, and to Jesus, the mediator of a new covenant" (Hebrews 12:22-24).

Those in the intermediate state now are the "spirits of the righteous made perfect." "Made perfect" means completely able to not sin. We won't have a body that lusts after the things of this world. Our spirit won't long to be reunited with the body that's decaying in the ground. There won't be spiritual enemies to tempt us. Nobody who desires to continue sinning will be there. All temptations will be gone.

Wow! Can we imagine what it will be like living without any guilt whatsoever? No. Guilt. Whatsoever. Forever.

We can't wait.

Stage 3 of Eternal Life: The Final State

Then there is the final state. Jesus promised the resurrection of our bodies. After the general resurrection, we'll enter the new heavens and earth. Jesus says in John 5:28-29, "An hour is coming when all who are in the tombs will hear [the Son of God's] voice and come out, those who have done good to the resurrection of life, and those who have done evil to the resurrection of judgment."[9]

Believers' bodies will be resurrected superior to what they are now. They will be raised imperishable and no longer subject to injuries and disease. First Corinthians 15:51-53 tells us that "we shall all be changed, in a moment, in the twinkling of an eye, at the last trumpet. For the trumpet will sound, and the dead will be raised imperishable, and we shall be changed. For this perishable body must put on the imperishable, and this mortal body must put on immortality." Our bodies will be raised in glory. Philippians 3:20-21 says that "our citizenship is in heaven, and...the Lord Jesus Christ...will transform our lowly body to be like his glorious body." First John 3:2 explains that when Jesus "appears we shall be like him."

Remember that when Jesus raised Lazarus, Lazarus came waddling out in his grave clothes (John 11:44). This instance was more of a reanimation rather than a resurrection in the full New Testament sense. By contrast, Jesus passed through His grave clothes, leaving them folded (John 20:6-7). He could enter locked rooms (John 20:19; 20:26), but He could also be hugged (John 20:16-17). Jesus ate (John 21:9-13) and has invited us to the marriage supper of the Lamb (Revelation 19:6-10). Believers are going to have resurrected bodies like Jesus' resurrected body.

GLORIOUS INHERITANCE 2: OUR HOME

Rarely does the media portray heaven as anything other than white with saints sitting on clouds, sporting flightless wings, strumming harps, and singing nonstop—forever.[10] Yuck.

In contrast, the book of Revelation describes the current state of heaven as colorful and filled with celestial creatures. Let's look in more detail how the Bible describes where we'll reside in our eternal state.

After the resurrection, God will create the new heavens and earth. We'll dwell in our glorious, resurrected bodies in the new heavens and earth. Some call this *final heaven.* Revelation 21:19-20 describes the new Jerusalem: "The foundations of the wall of the city were adorned with every kind of jewel," including jasper, sapphire, agate, emerald, onyx, carnelian, chrysolite, beryl, topaz, chrysoprase, jacinth, and amethyst. In other words, the city is jewel toned.

Our final abode won't be sitting on clouds. Rather, John tells us in Revelation 22:1-2, 4:

> The angel showed me the river of the water of life, bright as crystal, flowing from the throne of God and of the Lamb through the middle of the street of the city; also, on either side of the river, the tree of life with its twelve kinds of fruit, yielding its fruit each month. The leaves of the tree were for the healing of the nations...They will see his face, and his name will be on their foreheads.

Not only that, but Matthew 13:40-41 tells us that at the end of the age, "angels...will gather out of his kingdom all causes of sin and all law-breakers." No creature who doesn't want God's rule will be there.

GLORIOUS INHERITANCE 3: OUR FELLOWSHIP

Myth: We Won't Know Each Other in Heaven

Then there is the lie that we won't know each other in heaven. We (Clay and Jean) know a woman who was distraught after reading that she wouldn't know her recently deceased husband in heaven. But this idea comes from a misunderstanding of Isaiah 65:17: "Behold, I create new heavens and a new earth, and the former things shall not be remembered or come into mind." First, redeemed people are not "former things." We are eternal beings. Second, in the verse immediately prior, God says, "The former troubles are forgotten and are hidden from *my* eyes" (verse 16). Notice that it is referring to *God's* eyes. When God talks about forgetting and remembering things, He means that He is not going to call it to mind for the purpose of acting on it.

Being Together Forever

Atheist astronomer and science popularizer Carl Sagan's wife, Ann Druyan, talks about being with Carl while he was dying. She writes, "As we looked deeply into each other's eyes, it was with a shared conviction that our wondrous life together was ending forever."[11] They had no hope. How depressing. But sharing eternal life with our loved ones is the Christian hope. Paul writes 1 Thessalonians 4:13-18 to encourage us about our future reunion with loved ones:

> We do not want you to be uninformed, brothers, about those who are asleep, that you may not grieve as others do who have no hope. For since we believe that Jesus died and rose again, even so, through Jesus, God will bring with him those who have fallen asleep. For this we declare to you by a word from the Lord, that we who are alive, who are left until the coming of the Lord, will not precede those who have fallen asleep. For the Lord himself will descend from heaven with a cry of command, with the voice of an archangel, and with the sound of the trumpet of God. And the dead in Christ will rise first. Then we who are alive, who are left, will be caught up together with them in the clouds to meet the Lord in the air, and so we will always be with the Lord. Therefore encourage one another with these words.

Here "asleep" is a euphemism for death. Paul doesn't want Christians to grieve like the faithless. For when Jesus returns, "God will bring with" Jesus "those who have fallen asleep" (verse 14). There will be a command, an archangel's voice, and the sound of a trumpet, and Jesus will descend from heaven (verse 16). Angels will accompany him too (Mark 8:38; 2 Thessalonians 1:7). What a sight that will be!

Having heard Jesus' voice, "the dead in Christ will rise first" (verse 16; John 5:28-29)—their resurrected bodies will join with their spirits. Then, those in Christ who still live on earth will have their bodies transformed (1 Corinthians 15:52). Next, those alive on earth "will be caught up together" with those who rose first and are already with Jesus. They'll be reunited "together" with their departed loved ones in the clouds. They will "meet the Lord in the air, and so we will always be with the Lord" (verse 17).

Because this is our hope, Paul says, "Encourage one another with these words" (verse 18). Let's encourage our hearts and each other, dear reader. We'll have our minds. We won't have to recall anything we don't want to recall. But we will remember our loved ones and be with them for eternity.[12]

GLORIOUS INHERITANCE 4: OUR OCCUPATION

Myth: Our Only Occupation Will Be Singing Nonstop

In Mark Twain's *Adventures of Huckleberry Finn*, Miss Watson tells Huck "all about the good place. She said all a body would have to do there was to go around all day long with a harp and sing, forever and ever. So I didn't think too much of it. But I never said so."[13]

We will not be playing harps and singing nonstop. The idea that we'll sing nonstop comes from Revelation 4:8, which reads, "The four living creatures, each of them with six wings, are full of eyes all around and within, and day and night they never cease to say, 'Holy, holy, holy, is the Lord God Almighty, who was and is and is to come!' "

But humans don't and won't have six wings and eyes all over. So when this passage describes the four living creatures repeating this phrase, it's not talking about *people* singing forever. Plus, "never cease" doesn't mean repeat in a loop. The four living creatures also hold the golden bowls of saints' prayers (5:8), give commands (6:1, 3, 5, 7), sing other songs (5:8-10), and give items to angels (15:7). There's no doubt that we will sing—we will want to! But we won't sing nonstop in a loop.

Myth: Living Forever Would Be Boring

In the series finale of the NBC series *The Good Place* (2016–2020), several of the characters choose to be annihilated rather than stay in heaven. They choose annihilation because, as the show's star, Kristen Bell, tells *Entertainment Weekly*, "There's one line [in the series] that really sums it up. 'A vacation is only so fun because it has an ending.' If everything were bliss, *would* everyone be happy? I don't think so. Part of the drive and the passion is why it's the journey, not the destination."[14] In other words, eternal bliss is eternal boredom. This is typical of many people's conception of eternity. But in heaven we won't be on a never-ending vacation; rather, we will be given supremely valuable endeavors that we will *want* to do.

Banquets, Rejoicing, and Reigning

In eternity, we're not going to be on vacation. There will be plenty of banquets and rejoicing, but we will all have supremely meaningful, and thus, completely satisfying things to do. Our eternal occupation is reigning over God's kingdom (Revelation 22:5), which is supremely meaningful, and thus, supremely fulfilling.

Jean and I went on a speaking tour through Tokyo, Hong Kong, Kuala Lumpur, Singapore, and then back to Tokyo. We had a fabulous time. On our last night, after 23 nights away from home, we looked at each other in our Tokyo hotel room and wished out loud that they would ask us to keep on traveling and speaking—we would have welcomed it! I have spoken at conferences from London to Singapore, and not only do I not get tired of it, I don't see why I wouldn't want to do something like that forever.

GLORIOUS INHERITANCE 5: OUR GLORY

Not only will we have glorious, resurrected bodies and dwell on the beautiful new earth in fellowship with others who love God, but God intends to glorify us as well.

We Will Be Resplendent

Our resurrected bodies will be raised in glory and in power. First Corinthians 15:42-44, 47-48 explains:

> What is sown is perishable; what is raised is imperishable. It is sown in dishonor; it is raised in glory. It is sown in weakness; it is raised in power. It is sown a natural body; it is raised a spiritual body...The first man [Adam] was from the earth, a man of dust; the second man [Jesus] is from heaven. As was the man of dust, so also are those who are of the dust [Adam's descendants], and as is the man of heaven, so also are those who are of heaven [those born again].

The New Testament tells us that Christians will be glorified. The word *glory* often includes the idea of being luminous. Daniel 12:3 tells us, "Those who are wise will shine like the brightness of the heavens, and those who lead many to righteousness, like the stars for ever and ever" (NIV). In Zechariah 9:16, the Lord says about His people, "They will sparkle in his land like jewels in a crown" (NIV). Jesus reaffirms that when He says, "The righteous will shine like the sun in the kingdom of their Father" (Matthew 13:43).[15]

Luke 9:30-31 says that Moses and Elijah "appeared in glory." Professor Vern Poythress writes in *Theophany: A Biblical Theology of God's Appearing*, "In the consummation, we ourselves will reflect the glory associated with glory theophanies, such as the appearance of glory on the Mount of Transfiguration."[16] Alan W. Gomes asks, "What exactly do the biblical writers mean when they describe the resurrection body in such 'luminous language' or 'glowing terms'? Do they have in mind a literal, physical brightness similar to when Jesus stood transfigured before Peter, James, and John (Matt. 17:2)? Perhaps."[17]

We Will Be Renowned

Consider that autograph seekers might stand in line for hours, and sometimes pay a lot of money, to get the autograph of some star or celebrity. As Karon Warren puts it in *Investopedia,* "When you meet your favorite singer, actor, or sports figure, it can be thrilling. Naturally, you might want to commemorate this occasion by getting this person's signature."[18] In 2009, a signed photo of Albert Einstein was sold for $75,000. Babe Ruth's signature on a baseball went for $388,375 in 2012. Consider that the people buying these autographs rarely meet the celebrities themselves—they simply want something from them![19] Also, celebrities who sign their names rarely know the names of the people who are asking them for an autograph, and even if they hear their names, they probably don't remember them five minutes later. But the autograph seeker is thrilled to have had some interaction with the star.

One night on *The Tonight Show Starring Johnny Carson*, Frank Sinatra sat next to his good friend comedian Don Rickles. Sinatra asked Carson: "Can I tell a story about what this man did to me once?... It's a true story." Carson obliged and Sinatra continued, "I was eating dinner in a restaurant in New York, and I was sitting with some friends and [Rickles] came over to the table and he said, 'Frank, do me a favor will you? I'm sitting with a very pretty girl and, I'm trying to make out, you know, and I told her I know you and she really doesn't believe me. Would you stop by the table?' I said, 'All right.' "

Sinatra said that he soon went over to Rickles's table and said, "How are you, Don? It's nice to see you." But then, Sinatra laughed as he said Rickles blurted, "Can't you see I'm eating, Frank? What are you doing?" Sinatra, still laughing, then told the audience, "I went for the whole thing and stood there with my mouth open!"[20] Sinatra thought it was a funny story, and it is funny because it illustrates something important: We all want recognition from those who are important to us.

And who is more important than Jesus, our Savior, who is going to confess that He knows us? Revelation 3:5 says: "The one who conquers will be clothed thus in white garments, and I will never blot his name out of the book of life. I will confess his name before my Father and before his angels." Paige Patterson in his commentary on Revelation explains:

> A final portion of the promise to the conquerors is that Christ will confess their names in the presence of his Father and before his angels. Clothed in the white of holiness, the overcomer walks as worthy into the presence of God and the angels, unafraid of his name having been removed from the Book of Life; and he listens as Jesus confesses his name before all the cosmos.[21]

It's not only that we know Jesus; it's that Jesus knows us and is pleased for everyone to know that we have a special relationship. And there's so much more.

We Will Be Exalted

Jesus likens the kingdom of God to a nobleman who leaves his country to be crowned king. When he returns, he rewards those servants who put his money to work. To the one who doubles his money, he says, "Well done, good servant! Because you have been faithful in a very little, you shall have authority over ten cities" (Luke 19:17). It's possible those who've been the greatest servants on earth will rule over cities.

But won't that cause envy? No, for two reasons. First, in Matthew 20:25-28, Jesus explains what it takes to be exalted in His kingdom:

> You know that the rulers of the Gentiles lord it over them, and their great ones exercise authority over them. It shall not be so among you. But whoever would be great among you must be your servant, and whoever would be first among you must be your slave, even as the Son of Man came not to be served but to serve, and to give his life as a ransom for many.

If some are exalted, it won't be because of their speaking to large audiences or writing books; it will be because they were servants. We'll have seen their great servanthood in action—either on this earth or at the judgment—and will trust them to lead by serving as they rule under Jesus. Second, there won't be sin, which means there won't be envy. Everyone will have received their appropriate rewards when all is revealed. [22]

WHAT TO DO NOW: MEMORIZE VERSES ABOUT HEAVEN

Every night before we pray together, we recite a passage of Scripture. Usually, it has to do with eternity: Psalm 23, 2 Corinthians 4:16-18, Colossians 3:1-4, or Hebrews 12:1-3. We encourage you to memorize verses about heaven so they can encourage you during trying times.

A GLORIOUS ETERNITY AWAITS

With such a glorious inheritance awaiting us, we can now understand 2 Corinthians 4. In his second letter to the Corinthians, Paul tells of the suffering he has endured already: imprisonments, countless beatings, five floggings, stoned and left for dead, three shipwrecks, hunger and thirst, cold and exposed, and anxiety over the churches (2 Corinthians 11:23-29). But ahead of this, in 2 Corinthians 4:17-18, he writes: "For this light momentary affliction is preparing for us an eternal weight of glory beyond all comparison, as we look not to the things that are seen but to the things that are unseen. For the things that are seen are transient, but the things that are unseen are eternal." He calls being beaten, flogged, stoned, imprisoned, and shipwrecked a "light momentary affliction" in comparison to the glories to come. That's why he could persevere through suffering. That's why we can too.

A glorious eternity awaits.

Rejoice!

After Jesus sent out the 72 followers in Luke 10, we read in verses 17-18, "The seventy-two returned with joy, saying, 'Lord, even the demons are subject to us in your name!' And he said to them, 'I saw Satan fall like lightning from heaven.'" The disciples here rejoice that they can command powerful spiritual beings. But then, Jesus says something surprising in verse 20, "Nevertheless, do not rejoice in this, that the spirits are subject to you, but rejoice that your names are written in heaven." Jesus tells them that they shouldn't rejoice in being able to boss around beings so powerful that they could twist the strongest of men into pretzels. Rather, Jesus says that His disciples should rejoice that their names are written in the book of life. This is the Christian hope!

If we're not supposed to rejoice in being able to command powerful spiritual beings, how much less should we rejoice in the size of our breasts or biceps, the size of our 401(k)s, our titles and honors, our companies, or our accomplishments? None of these things are inherently valuable. Former Navy SEAL Chad Williams puts this in perspective:

> *We made it!* I thought when the Navy SEAL trident was pinned onto the left chest of my uniform for the first time. All the work, all the physical and mental perseverance… had all led to that moment when I received the insignia that let everyone who saw it know I was officially a SEAL. I had done what I said I would do. I had accomplished my "big thing."[23]

But, writes Chad, after receiving his trident, as he was driving home to Huntington Beach for his graduation party, "That trip home became one of the saddest times of my life."[24] Becoming a SEAL was an amazing accomplishment, but it wasn't eternally valuable.

What *is* eternally valuable is that we Christians are going to live forever with glorious resurrected bodies in the beautiful new heavens and earth. We should rejoice that we are going to live forever! And we are going to be forever *together*. Remember that the most famous verse in the Bible, John 3:16, ends with "shall not perish but have eternal life" (NIV).

WHAT TO DO NOW: REJOICE OVER YOUR ETERNAL FUTURE

Take a moment now to thank God that you're going to live forever with a glorious resurrected body in the beautiful new heavens and earth. Rejoice that you'll be together with loved ones in Jesus' presence for eternity.

Focus on the Glory to Come

It's impossible to overemphasize the importance of focusing on the glory of eternal life in times of suffering. In fact, Paul says that the suffering we endure is nothing compared to the glory that awaits us: "I consider that the sufferings of this present time are not worth comparing with the glory that is to be revealed to us" (Romans 8:18). Second Corinthians 4:16-18 is worth quoting one last time:

> We do not lose heart. Though our outer self is wasting away, our inner self is being renewed day by day. For this light momentary affliction is preparing for us an eternal weight of glory beyond all comparison, as we look not to the things that are seen but to the things that are unseen. For the things that are seen are transient, but the things that are unseen are eternal.

In his commentary on this passage, Murray Harris explains, "Christians should be characterized by a fixation on invisible, eternal realities. Paradoxically, their eyes are riveted on what cannot be seen. The world of sense does not determine their outlook and action."[25] Indeed, Hebrews 11:1 defines faith: "Faith is confidence in what we hope for and assurance about what we do not see" (NIV). Dear reader, if you are already focused on the glories of eternity, then you will be able to honorably endure suffering while awaiting your deliverance. But if you are not presently focused on the glories of eternity, then our Lord will employ suffering to change your focus.

One hundred years of suffering on earth is dwarfed to insignificance by our glorious eternity. Is there a loved one you look forward to seeing in heaven? If so, consider that you could spend an eternity with that loved one without reducing by one second the amount of time you have to do anything else. Remembering that we are going to be together for eternity helps us be victorious amid suffering.

"Eternity's Still Okay"

The major help to facing our sufferings here is that we're going to be together for eternity. In September 2001, Lisa Beamer was a mother of two and pregnant with a third when terrorists hijacked and crashed United Airlines flight 93 in Pennsylvania. Her husband, Todd Beamer, was on that flight and famously said, "Let's roll," before the plane crashed. Lisa says that on September 11 she was numb, and "What prevented me from hysteria was knowing the truth—in the end it was still okay." She writes, "I said over and over and still do: Eternity's still okay, even if here and now isn't. The foundations of my life are still intact."[26]

When I (Clay), first read Lisa Beamer's eternal perspective, I was shocked. I wondered, *Where did she get such maturity?* Well, she explains, " 'This life isn't all there is,' Mom repeatedly told us kids. 'It's merely a drop in the bucket. We're here to prepare ourselves for eternity and to help other people do the same. Life isn't easy, but the good news is that, even at its best, it can't compare to how great heaven is going to be.' "[27] Indeed, Lisa Beamer is victorious, and we can be too, knowing that no matter how bad things get here, the foundations of our Christian lives are still intact: We're all going to be together for eternity!

No more death or mourning or crying or pain. All gone. A glorious eternity awaits.

10

THE EXALTED STATUS OF THE VICTOR

The Bible says that we relate to God in many ways. For example, He is the Shepherd and we are the sheep (John 10:1-16). He is the Vine and we are the branches (John 15:1-11). We even relate to Him as a friend (John 15:13-15). Those are analogies. But the Bible also uses the most exalted of all human relationships. It teaches that we relate to God as a son and as a bride/wife. Those who honor God through suffering will enjoy the exalted privilege of being a son of God and the bride/wife of Jesus throughout eternity. The earthly father/son and husband/wife relationships are analogies for the real thing in heaven. We are sons of the heavenly Father and the bride of Christ literally. We are not *like* sons to the Father. We *are* sons of the Father. Similarly, we are not *like* brides to Christ; we *are* the bride of Christ.[1]

We'll explore these blessings in this chapter, but first we need to understand a common problem: Satan strives to destroy the God-ordained family so that we won't comprehend the blessings that await.

That the Bible tells us we relate to God as a child relates to a father helps many understand His good care and love. But it can confuse those who have absent or ungodly fathers. Many perceive either the

Father or Jesus in a way similar to their perceptions of their earthly father or earthly husband.

For example, those with absent fathers tend to think of God as distant and uncaring. Those with angry, vengeful, cynical, or unloving dads tend to treat God as if He's the same way. One woman told Jean that she thought her earthly dad was a better father than God because she had her dad wrapped around her little finger, but God wasn't answering prayers the way she wanted.

When I (Jean) first became a Christian, I wrongly assumed that the Father and Jesus had traits similar to my earthly dad's traits. Once I realized this, I located verses that described them differently, and I wrote out the verses to memorize them. For example, Hebrews 11:6 assured me God wanted to hear from me: "Without faith it is impossible to please him, for whoever would draw near to God must believe that he exists and that he rewards those who seek him." Additionally, I began prayers with "My Father who art in heaven and who is not my earthly dad" to remind myself to approach God according to what Scripture said. Then, I thanked Him for His love and good care. In time, the mistaken notions disappeared.

Similarly, if a wife's husband is unloving or unfaithful, she may find it difficult to enthusiastically appreciate Jesus as the bridegroom. Further, Satan has lately inspired many to consider marriage to be misogynistic at its root. "When you peel back the layers of history and propaganda," writes Clementine Ford about marriage, "it's impossible not to want to completely destroy this inherently misogynistic institution."[2] Ford continues, "Marriage is an unsalvageable lie, designed to keep women in service to patriarchy and away from realising our full potential."[3] Let's be clear: This line of thinking is Satan's work and shows the need for fathers and husbands to be Christlike.

WHAT TO DO NOW: CORRECT FALSE BELIEFS

So, dear Christian, if you too have mistaken notions about God as the Father or Jesus as bridegroom, then take steps like Jean took: Write out and memorize verses that correct your false beliefs. And as we encouraged in the introduction, "Preparing to Conquer," pray for revelation of the glory that awaits us forever because of our intimate relationship with God the Father and Jesus the Bridegroom.

ENJOY OUR RELATIONSHIP AS SONS

The first major blessing given to the victorious overcomer is that we are sons of God who will inherit all things. Jesus says, in John 1:12, that "to all who did receive him, who believed in his name, he gave the right to become children of God." In Ephesians 1:3, Paul says, "Blessed be the God and Father of our Lord Jesus Christ, who has blessed us in Christ with every spiritual blessing in the heavenly places." We've been given *every spiritual blessing* in the heavenly places! Every. Spiritual. Blessing. Then, only one sentence later, he says, "In love he predestined us for adoption to himself as sons through Jesus Christ, according to the purpose of his will, to the praise of his glorious grace, with which he has blessed us in the Beloved" (verses 4-6). Of course, in this *mean*time, it's tough. Presently, we "groan inwardly as we wait eagerly for adoption as sons, the redemption of our bodies. For in this hope we were saved" (Romans 8:23-24). Galatians 4:4-7 tells us that "God sent forth his Son...so that we might receive adoption as sons. And because you are sons, God has sent the Spirit of his Son into our hearts, crying, 'Abba! Father!' So you are no longer a slave, but a son, and if a son, then an heir through God."

But sadly, for many Christians, there is this blah-blah-blah factor—a sort of, "Yeah, I know, we're the sons of God, blah, blah, blah." And some Christians wonder if adoption as a son into God's family isn't much less than adoption into a rich person's family here on earth. Some may think, *I'd rather be adopted by [insert the name of your favorite rich and famous person here]; then that would really be something.* But they would be wrong. We may not see the fullness of our adoption as children into God's family yet, but it's coming! Let's look at the blessings of being children of God.

We Take His Name

The first blessing of being a son is that we take His name. All adopted kids do this. Can you imagine a parent adopting an older child who says, "Great, you can adopt me, but I'm not taking your name"? Of course not. Thus, we believers in Jesus as the Christ (Anointed One) call ourselves "Christians." In Acts 11:26, we read that "in Antioch the disciples were first called Christians." In Colossians 3:17, Paul tells us, "Whatever you do, in word or deed, do everything in the name of the Lord Jesus." Do we understand our privilege, dear Christian, of acting on behalf of Jesus? The privilege of representing Jesus to others? As Paul writes in 2 Corinthians 5:20, "We are ambassadors for Christ, God making his appeal through us."

Taking His name brings three major obligations. First, don't bring shame on the family name. This is what Paul says the Jews did when, in Romans 2:24, he writes, "The name of God is blasphemed among the Gentiles because of you." Second, don't disown the family name. As Jesus says in Matthew 10:32-33: "Everyone who acknowledges me before men, I also will acknowledge before my Father who is in heaven, but whoever denies me before men, I also will deny before my Father who is in heaven." Clearly, if we deny being Christians, then we are denying that we belong to God's family. Third, rejoice; revel in the fact that you represent the name of Jesus. Consider that an ambassador of the United States has great influence and great respect (at least most places). Mistreating an ambassador is considered equivalent to mistreating the country. Same with us. We represent the King of kings and the Lord of lords. Anyone who mistreats us will be held accountable at judgment.[4] What a privilege to represent Jesus.

We Share His Suffering

This might seem like an odd "blessing," but it is a blessing. Consider Philippians 1:29: "It has been *granted* to you that for the sake of Christ you should not only believe in him but also suffer for his sake." The word "granted" in that passage means that God has given us the privilege of suffering on Jesus' behalf.[5] It's a blessing of grace from God for us to suffer for Jesus.

Here are two human examples. First, many men are awed by this or that sports star. If after a game at a stadium, a fan's favorite sports star asked him to help carry the star's gear to their car, the guy would not only do it, he would tell everyone he knows about meeting this sports star and carrying their gear to their car. In the same way, it's a privilege for us to help carry Jesus' burden. Second, most men who stormed the Normandy beaches on D-Day were proud of it. One such soldier is Ray Wallace, a former paratrooper with the 82nd Airborne Division. He parachuted in and was captured by the Germans within a month. Reflecting back, he said, "I guess you can say I'm proud of what I did but I didn't do that much."[6] Wallace was proud that he suffered for others.

So again, Paul writes in Romans 8:17, "If we are children, then we are heirs—heirs of God and co-heirs with Christ, if indeed we share in his sufferings in order that we may also share in his glory" (NIV). Notice that we must share in Jesus' suffering to share in His glory. As the saying goes, "No guts, no glory." Or, as Quaker William Penn, the founder of Pennsylvania, famously put it, "No pain, no palm; no thorns, no throne; no gall, no glory; no cross, no crown."[7]

Every member of a family shares the problems of that family. If you're born into a poor family in a very poor country such as South Sudan, you share in the family's problems. On the other hand, if you're born into the British Royal Family, you must contend with the tabloid headlines about various Royal family members. And if you're born into God's family you suffer the problems of His family. But could there be any greater sign that you are a member of God's family than that you suffer the problems of His family? Presently, many people hate and slander our Lord and therefore hate and slander us. But don't worry, one of these days soon He's going to come back and clear His name—and we'll be there!

We Enjoy Confidence Before Him

One of the blessings of being a son is that sons have immediate access to and confidence before their fathers. Assuming their relationship is healthy, they can go right in and talk to dad any time they want. They know that their father will welcome them. As mentioned earlier, Romans 8:15 tells us that we have "the Spirit of adoption as sons, by whom we cry, 'Abba! Father!' "

But Christians must be careful. There is, again, the blah-blah-blah factor that can be stumbled into. Christians may think something like, *Yes, I know we can talk to our heavenly Father just like we can talk to our earthly father; blah, blah, blah.* I've heard Christians say things like, "God is my best bud," "God's my pal," and "God's so cute." Some even call Him "dude." He may be our Father, but He is also the Creator of the universe and the one to whom we will give an account.

In *The Chronicles of Narnia*, C.S. Lewis well illustrates the significance of who Jesus is when Mr. and Mrs. Beaver describe Aslan (a type for Jesus):

> "I tell you he is the King of the wood and the son of the great Emperor-Beyond-the-Sea. Don't you know who is the King of Beasts? Aslan is a lion—*the* Lion, the great Lion."

"Ooh!" said Susan, "I'd thought he was a man. Is he—quite safe? I shall feel rather nervous about meeting a lion."

"That you will, dearie, and no mistake," said Mrs. Beaver. "If there's anyone who can appear before Aslan without their knees knocking, they're either braver than most or else just silly."

"Then he isn't safe?" said Lucy.

"Safe?" said Mr. Beaver. "Don't you hear what Mrs. Beaver tells you? Who said anything about safe? 'Course he isn't safe. But he's good. He's the King, I tell you."[8]

Yes, the Lord is our Father, but we need to remember to whom we're talking. Dallas Willard puts it well,

> The intelligent person recognizes that his or her well-being lies in being in harmony with God and what God is doing in the "kingdom." God is not mean, but he is dangerous. It is the same with other great forces he has placed in reality. Electricity and nuclear power, for example, are not mean, but they are dangerous. One who does not, in a certain sense, "worry" about God, simply isn't smart.[9]

We don't treat the Lord as "dude" or "cute." Revelation 4:2-5 describes the Lord on His throne.

> A throne stood in heaven, with one seated on the throne. And he who sat there had the appearance of jasper and carnelian, and around the throne was a rainbow that had the appearance of an emerald. Around the throne were twenty-four thrones, and seated on the thrones were

> twenty-four elders, clothed in white garments, with golden crowns on their heads. From the throne came flashes of lightning, and rumblings and peals of thunder, and before the throne were burning seven torches of fire, which are the seven spirits of God.

We Inherit His Kingdom

That we Christians inherit the kingdom of our Father follows logically. Children inherit from their parents. Romans 8:16-17 explains: "The Spirit himself bears witness with our spirit that we are children of God, and if children, then heirs—heirs of God and fellow heirs with Christ, provided we suffer with him in order that we may also be glorified with him." Suffering reproach for the name of Christ is evidence that we really are His children. If we are His children, then our Father will give us the kingdom.

Throughout history sons have inherited kingdoms from their fathers. John writes in Revelation 21:5-7:

> He who sits on the throne said, "Behold, I am making all things new." And He said, "Write, for these words are faithful and true." Then He said to me, "It is done. I am the Alpha and the Omega, the beginning and the end. I will give to the one who thirsts from the spring of the water of life without cost. He who *overcomes* will *inherit these things*, and I will be his God and he will be My son" (NASB1995).

There it is again—those who overcome persecutions, hardships, temptations, and sufferings will inherit all things "and I will be his God and he will be My son." Remember, dear Christian, that either this is true or it is not. If it is not true, then Christianity is a waste of time. But if it is true, then we've been adopted as sons and will inherit the kingdom!

In Luke 12:35-36, Jesus says, "Stay dressed for action and keep your lamps burning, and be like men who are waiting for their master to come home from the wedding feast, so that they may open the door to him at once when he comes and knocks." Six verses later, Jesus says, "Who then is the faithful and wise manager, whom his master will set over his household, to give them their portion of food at the proper time? Blessed is that servant whom his master will find so doing when he comes. Truly, I say to you, he will set him over all his possessions" (verses 42-44). We will be in charge, we will oversee "all his possessions."

That we'll reign brings meaning to Luke 12:32: "Fear not, little flock, for it is your Father's good pleasure to give you the kingdom." We aren't visitors or even long-term tenants; we're owners.

The South Coast Plaza is less than 20 minutes from where we live in Orange County, California, and we suspect that none of the glitzier brands are absent from that mall. There's Giorgio Armani, Cartier, Chanel, Jimmy Choo, Dior, Gucci, Prada, and the list goes on. One day we were walking the plaza, and in a store window there was a beautiful necklace adorned with dozens of diamonds and emeralds and we don't know what else, but it was beautiful. Out of curiosity we asked the saleswoman its price, and she replied, "Six hundred thousand dollars." We thought the necklace beautiful, but we're thankful to say, we realize that we'll be getting things much better than that in the kingdom to come, so we honestly had no desire to own it. After all, all things are ours!

We Share in His Judging

Paul writes in 1 Corinthians 6:2-3, "Do you not know that the saints will judge the world? And if the world is to be judged by you, are you incompetent to try trivial cases? Do you not know that we are to judge angels? How much more, then, matters pertaining to this life!" Note that we are to judge the world and angels.

Judging the world and angels refers, of course, to judging rebellious humans and rebellious angels at the judgment. With Jesus we'll condemn rebellious humans and angels as deserving their fate of exclusion from God and His people. This is exemplified by Jesus in Luke 11:31-32:

> The queen of the South will rise up at the judgment with the men of this generation and condemn them, for she came from the ends of the earth to hear the wisdom of Solomon, and behold, something greater than Solomon is here. The men of Nineveh will rise up at the judgment with this generation and condemn it, for they repented at the preaching of Jonah, and behold, something greater than Jonah is here.

Notice that both the queen and the people of Nineveh repented of their sins with less evidence for the truth about God than the people of Jesus' day. Thus, they can stand up at the judgment and condemn the people who had personally witnessed Jesus' miracles but refused to repent.

With this in view, Revelation 3:21-22 makes sense: "The one who conquers, I will grant him to sit with me on my throne, as I also conquered and sat down with my Father on his throne. He who has an ear, let him hear what the Spirit says to the churches." About this G.K. Beale writes, "Christ promises that if those in the church overcome pressures to accommodate to idolatry and resist taking a low profile in their witness, they will inherit a ruling position with him."[10] Grant Osborne points out that "the conquerors will not just sit on their own thrones but will share Christ's throne."[11] Osborne continues:

> There is a three-stage development in the throne theology of the Bible. In the OT it is Yahweh who sits on the

> throne in majesty and judgment. In the Gospels Jesus as Son of Man partakes of God's throne, also in majesty and judgment (Matt. 19:28; 25:31-46). The same is true in the Apocalypse. In chapter 4 Yahweh is on his glorious throne, and in chapter 5 Jesus in his redemptive work is enthroned with him. Finally, in Matt. 19:28 (par. Luke 22:29, 30); 1 Cor. 6:2; 2 Tim. 2:12a, as well as Rev. 2:26-27; 3:21; and 20:4, the victorious saints also share in the throne of glory and judgment.[12]

Christians who endure suffering by faithfully continuing to honor God tacitly indict Satan and his angels who rebelled against God, even though they saw God's face. Thus, as mentioned above, Christians will be qualified to judge the world and even angels (1 Corinthians 6:2-3).

We Share in His Reign

We share Jesus' kingdom and will share His occupation. What's Jesus' occupation? In Revelation 11:15, we read, "Then the seventh angel blew his trumpet, and there were loud voices in heaven, saying, 'The kingdom of the world has become the kingdom of our Lord and of his Christ, and he shall reign forever and ever.' " Jesus reigns. Our occupation is the same as His—we will reign with Him. Second Timothy 2:11-13 is an amazing passage:

> Here is a trustworthy saying:
>
> If we died with him,
> we will also live with him;
> if we endure,
> we will also reign with him.
> If we disown him,

> he will also disown us;
> if we are faithless,
> he remains faithful,
> for he cannot disown himself (NIV).

Notice that in verse 11, Paul writes, "If we endure, we will also reign with him." There it is again: If we continue to honor God through whatever tribulation or suffering the world or the devil may throw at us, then we will reign with Him. This is so important that in verse 14 Paul adds, "Keep reminding God's people of these things" (NIV). Paul says to keep reminding each other of this true saying that was shared among the early church.

That we Christians will rule harkens back to Daniel 7:22: "The Ancient of Days came, and judgment was given for the saints of the Most High, and the time came when the saints possessed the kingdom." So God's people will possess the kingdom. Verse 27 reads, "Then the sovereignty, power and greatness of all the kingdoms under heaven will be handed over to the holy people of the Most High. His kingdom will be an everlasting kingdom, and all rulers will worship and obey him" (NIV). That's us!

Revelation 22:1-5 reads:

> The angel showed me the river of the water of life, bright as crystal, flowing from the throne of God and of the Lamb through the middle of the street of the city; also, on either side of the river, the tree of life with its twelve kinds of fruit, yielding its fruit each month. The leaves of the tree were for the healing of the nations. No longer will there be anything accursed, but the throne of God and of the Lamb will be in it, and his servants will worship him. They will see his face, and his name will be on their foreheads. And night will be no more. They will need no

> light of lamp or sun, for the Lord God will be their light, and they will reign forever and ever.[13]

We are inheriting the kingdom so that we can reign over it.

ENJOY OUR RELATIONSHIP AS BRIDE/WIFE

We are sons of God with all the blessings that brings, but there's more than that. We are also the bride of Christ. Paul writes, " 'Therefore a man shall leave his father and mother and hold fast to his wife, and the two shall become one flesh.' This mystery is profound, and I am saying that it refers to Christ and the church" (Ephesians 5:31-32). The book of Revelation describes the saints as a whole being Jesus' bride. Revelation 21:9-11 (NIV) reads,

> One of the seven angels who had the seven bowls full of the seven last plagues came and said to me, "Come, I will show you the bride, the wife of the Lamb." And he carried me away in the Spirit to a mountain great and high, and showed me the Holy City, Jerusalem, coming down out of heaven from God. It shone with the glory of God, and its brilliance was like that of a very precious jewel, like a jasper, clear as crystal.[14]

The Jerusalem that comes down from heaven has sometimes been thought of as only a city. But Jesus isn't marrying a city. We are the bride of Christ![15]

Being the bride of Christ means that there are many more blessings to enjoy.

We Share in the Marriage Supper of the Lamb

Revelation 19:9 reads, "Blessed are those who are invited to the marriage supper of the Lamb." In Jesus' day, a wedding banquet ideally lasted seven days and was a time of joy and celebration. Imagine attending the wedding banquet of Jesus! And, yes, we will actually be eating food and drinking wine. After all, in His post-resurrection body, Jesus ate fish (Luke 24:41-43) and even cooked and served His disciples a breakfast of bread and fish (John 21:9-13). As to wine, when Jesus gave the cup of wine to His disciples at the Last Supper, He said, "I tell you I will not drink again of this fruit of the vine until that day when I drink it new with you in my Father's kingdom" (Matthew 26:29).

That celebrations before and with the Lord involve good food and good drink finds expression in Deuteronomy 14:25-26: "Exchange your tithe for silver, and take the silver with you and go to the place the LORD your God will choose. Use the silver to buy whatever you like: cattle, sheep, wine or other fermented drink, or anything you wish. Then you and your household shall eat there in the presence of the LORD your God and rejoice" (NIV). In Psalm 104:15, David blesses the Lord for giving "wine to gladden the heart of man." Although the Lord opposes the misuse of pleasure, He does not oppose pleasure itself. In fact, He made all the pleasures for us to enjoy! Consider Psalm 16:11, "You make known to me the path of life; in your presence there is fullness of joy; at your right hand are pleasures forevermore." The Lord is pro-pleasure and, as we just read, there will be pleasure in just being with Him: "in your presence there is fullness of joy."

Contrary to the notion that being with Jesus will be a joyless, sterile event, consider that Jesus ate and drank so often with sinners that the Pharisees falsely accused Him of being "a glutton and a drunkard" (Matthew 11:19). Those in heaven will be like Him. Now, we have no desire to encourage anyone to drink wine, but we must be honest about this because it runs counter to the comment, "It's so pleasurable that it must be sinful" (we suspect that the first one to say that was the devil, and he has been disseminating that talking point to his minions ever since). The misrepresentation that God is anti-pleasure here on earth makes Christians fear eternity in heaven. But, again, the Lord isn't against pleasure. He made food, drink, sex, and all other pleasure possible.

Further, we're going to enjoy banqueting with Jesus and each other. Revelation 19:6 tells us this: "I heard what seemed to be the voice of a great multitude, like the roar of many waters and like the sound of mighty peals of thunder, crying out, 'Hallelujah! For the Lord our God the Almighty reigns.'" Why this exultation? Verses 7-9 tell us:

> "Let us rejoice and exult
> and give him the glory,
> for the marriage of the Lamb has come,
> and his Bride has made herself ready;
> it was granted her to clothe herself
> with fine linen, bright and pure"—
> for the fine linen is the righteous deeds of the saints.
>
> And the angel said to me, "Write this: Blessed are those who are invited to the marriage supper of the Lamb." And he said to me, "These are the true words of God."

Osborne writes, "For the saints, it is the greatest celebration of them all, for they will become the 'bride of the Lamb,' and all of heaven is their dowry."[16]

What's the feast going to be like? In Luke 12:37, Jesus says, "Blessed are those servants whom the master finds awake when he comes. Truly, I say to you, he will dress himself for service and have them recline at table, and he will come and serve them."[17]

Wow, Jesus will dress Himself to serve us. We wonder how He will be dressed.

The night before Clay had a procedure at Cedars-Sinai, we decided to treat ourselves to a dinner at Wolfgang Puck's restaurant Spago. All the servers were dressed in black except one who wore a multi-colored pastel jacket. He came by our table to ask how we were doing and if we needed anything. He was friendly, and we chatted a while. We asked what he did, and he replied that he was the director of food and beverage for all of Wolfgang's restaurants throughout the world. A few days later, Clay Googled the restaurant and discovered he was Wolfgang's 29-year-old son. We really liked him, he was specially dressed and served us well, but we expect that Jesus will be much, much better dressed than even that. We will be talking not to Wolfgang Puck's son, Byron, but to the King of kings and Lord of lords.

Also, Luke 12:37 says that Jesus will have us recline at the table. Jesus will have us comfortably seated. Not like the hard plastic chairs in fast food restaurants. Jesus intends to make us comfortable, and we have every reason to believe He will succeed.

Finally, it says that Jesus will serve us. This last part amazes Jean and me. Jesus will serve us? Nowhere in our human experience that we know of do kings or presidents personally serve those at a banquet. We're reminded of Jesus' saying, "The greatest among you shall be your servant" (Matthew 23:11). Jesus is going to take care of our desires—His goal will be to make us happy!

And what are we going to eat? Isaiah 25:6 describes a coming meal, "On this mountain the LORD of hosts will make for all peoples a feast of rich food, a feast of well-aged wine, of rich food full of marrow, of aged wine well refined." Expect the best wine anyone has ever tasted and food of a quality along the lines of something like Wagyu beef.[18] And there will be all we could hope for.

We Share His Life

Jean and I are thankful that we have spent many years together and we share each other's lives. We are individuals—Jean's a technology-oriented perfectionist, and I am more of a conceptual, big-picture person—but we are one in so many ways. When we first started going out, I would point to a chair or a painting or a car or whatever and tell Jean how much I liked it, but Jean would (nicely) tell me how she didn't like it and then point to something she liked better, which I didn't like. Frankly, sometimes I got a little hurt. But after decades together, we usually like the same furniture, art, TV shows, movies, and so on. Now we don't like everything the same. For example, Jean likes eating game (elk, deer, rabbit, etc.), of which I'm not a big fan. But on the whole, we like the same food prepared in the same ways. When we were younger, Jean didn't like history, but I did. Now we both love it. We are both writers and speakers, and we share many interests. Jean enjoys cozy mysteries, while I'd rather be watching a Jason Bourne-type of movie. (In all fairness, Jean does like Bourne movies, and I can tolerate the occasional cozy mystery if there's nothing else on TV.) Likewise, in sharing Jesus' life, we will share His interests, plans, and purposes, but we will still be ourselves.

Wives share in the possessions and dignity of their husbands. The union between a man and his wife illustrates the spiritual union we have with Jesus in all its fullness in the kingdom. G.K. Beale says, "The meaning of the marriage analogy...is the consummate communion of God with his people."[19]

There will be much more of a oneness with Jesus and each other. As Jesus prays in John 17:20-23:

> I do not ask for these only, but also for those who will believe in me through their word, that they may all be one, just as you, Father, are in me, and I in you, that they also may be in us, so that the world may believe that you have sent me. The glory that you have given me I have given to them, that they may be one even as we are one, I in them and you in me, that they may become perfectly one, so that the world may know that you sent me and loved them even as you loved me.

We Are Going to Enjoy Him and Each Other Forever

Our going through suffering here is how the Lord prepares us to be a bride beautifully dressed for her husband. G.K. Beale points out, "Preparation of the 'bride adorned *for* her *husband*' conveys the thought of God's preparation of His people for Himself. Throughout history God is forming His people to be His bride, so that they will reflect His glory in the ages to come (so Eph. 5:25-27), an idea developed in what remains of Revelation 21 (cf. 2 Cor. 11:2)."[20]

Although some in today's audience might consider it corny, The Dixie Cups came out with a song in 1964 about a woman getting married entitled "Chapel of Love." In that song, young women sing about the joy of going to the chapel where they're going to get married![21] The point of the song is that each woman is thrilled at the prospect of getting married to the man of her dreams.

When "Chapel of Love" debuted, it knocked the Beatles out of the number 1 spot on the *Billboard* Hot 100. *Rolling Stone* ranked it number 284 on the list of "The 500 Greatest Songs of All Time."[22] In 1972, Bette Midler did a cover of the song, which was remastered in 2016 and hit 40 on *Billboard*. Then, The Beach Boys did a cover of the song in 1976 (remastered 2000). Elton John did a version of it for the 1994 movie *Four Weddings and a Funeral*. It has also been featured in films such as *Full Metal Jacket* (1987) and *Father of the Bride* (1991).[23] Much more could be said, but the point is made: People resonate with the song because brides are thrilled about getting married.[24] How much more should we Christians, the bride of Christ, greatly exult in the marriage supper of the Lamb?

We're going to the chapel, and we're going to get married.

"And the angel said to me, 'Write this: Blessed are those who are invited to the marriage supper of the Lamb.' And he said to me, 'These are the true words of God'" (Revelation 19:9).

CONCLUSION

VICTORY IN SUFFERING AND ETERNAL GLORY

In Revelation chapters 2 and 3, we read Jesus' messages of warning and encouragement to seven churches: Ephesus, Smyrna, Pergamum, Thyatira, Sardis, Philadelphia, and Laodicea. Jesus warns five of these seven churches against sexual immortality, idolatrous compromise, doctrinal aberration, failure to witness, and lovelessness. But Jesus tells all seven churches that if they conquer—if they continue to honor Jesus in suffering, temptations, trials, and even death—then they will be eternally rewarded.

Let's look at what He says to only the church at Smyrna in Revelation 2. Jesus has no criticism of that church but commends them in verse 9: "I know your afflictions and your poverty—yet you are rich! I know about the slander of those who say they are Jews and are not, but are a synagogue of Satan" (NIV). Thus, the Smyrnaeans were poor and suffering, but they were victorious because they honored God through it. In fact, Jesus says to this impoverished church, "You are rich." Jesus says that because at His second coming they will inherit the kingdom. Jesus encourages them in verse 10, "Do not be afraid of what you are about to suffer. I tell you, the devil will put some of you in prison to test you, and you will suffer persecution... Be faithful, even to the point of death, and I will give you life as your victor's crown" (NIV). Even if we are killed, we are the victor. This is followed in verse 11 by a divine "listen up": "He who has an ear, let him hear what the Spirit says to the churches." So let us pay close attention to what Jesus says next, "The one who conquers will not be hurt by the second death."[1]

There it is. If we, like the Smyrnaeans, honor God through whatever the world and the devil throw at us, whether it be tribulation, poverty, sickness, slander, the plundering of our property,[2] imprisonment, or even death, then we conquer, we are victorious, and we will not be hurt by the second death. In short, we gain eternal life.

Thankfully, we have a historical example of someone from Smyrna who did just that. Polycarp was a disciple of the apostle John and became bishop of Smyrna around AD 115. Thirty to forty years later, he was burned at the stake. The Roman governor told him prior to his death that he would be executed if he did not give a public, token acknowledgement to Caesar as Lord.[3] The magistrate tried to persuade Polycarp, "saying …, 'Swear by the genius of Caesar; repent and say, "Away with the atheists."' Then Polycarp with solemn countenance looked upon the whole multitude of lawless heathen that were in the stadium, and waved his hand to them; and groaning and looking up to heaven he said, 'Away with the atheists.' "[4] In response, "the magistrate pressed him hard and said, 'Swear the oath, and I will release you; revile the Christ.' " But Polycarp replied, "Eighty-six years have I been His servant, and He has done me no wrong. How then can I blaspheme my King who saved me?"[5] But the magistrate persisted saying, "Swear by the genius of Caesar." To that Polycarp answered, "If you suppose vainly that I will swear by the genius of Caesar, as you say, and feign that you are ignorant who I am, hear you plainly: I am a Christian. But if you would learn the doctrine of Christianity, assign a day and give me a hearing."[6] Hence they bound Polycarp to a stake, and among other praises to God Polycarp looked up to heaven and said,

> I bless You because You have granted me this day and hour, that I might receive a portion amongst the number of martyrs in the cup of Your Christ unto resurrection of eternal life, both of soul and of body, in the incorruptibility of the Holy Spirit. May I be received among these in Your presence this day, as a rich and acceptable sacrifice, as You did prepare and reveal it beforehand, and have accomplished it, You that [are] the faithful and true God. For this cause, yea and for all things, I praise You, I bless You, I glorify You, through the eternal and heavenly High-priest, Jesus Christ, Your beloved Son, through Whom, with Him and the Holy Spirit, be glory both now and ever and for the ages to come. Amen.[7]

When Polycarp had finished his prayer, his accusers lit a fire, but the flames billowed such that they weren't consuming him, so they ordered an executioner to stab him with a dagger and thus Polycarp died.[8]

But, of course, that's not the end. As Polycarp writes, "For if we be well pleasing unto Him in this present world, we shall receive the future world also, according as He promised us to raise us from the dead, and that if we conduct ourselves worthily of Him *we shall also reign with Him*, if indeed we have faith."[9] Indeed. Polycarp now reigns with Jesus and all the saints forever and ever.

Similarly, if we honor God through suffering, even to the plundering of our property, imprisonment, and death, we will inherit life as a reward for our continuing to honor Jesus in spite of great suffering. Paige Patterson in his commentary on Revelation is correct: "Although sometimes difficult for humans to appreciate adequately, the Scriptures seem to make clear that for every injustice and evil suffered by believers on the earth, there is significant reward in heaven. Here is a promise that because of the conditions of poverty and tribulation through which Smyrnaean believers were walking, their value in God's eyes was exponentially increasing."[10]

Victory over suffering here on planet Earth is central to reigning forever. In Revelation 21:7, God says, "Those who are *victorious* will inherit all this, and I will be their God and they will be my children" (NIV). Similarly, Jesus in Revelation 3:21 promises, "To the one who is *victorious*, I will give the right to sit with me on my throne, just as I was victorious and sat down with my Father on his throne" (NIV).

Our kingdom awaits, and we will reign over it!

APPENDIX

ANSWERS TO COMMON QUESTIONS

1. SHOULD I GET A SECOND OPINION ON HEALTH-RELATED PROBLEMS?

If you have an unusual ailment, we urge you to get a second opinion from a *teaching* hospital. Both 23 years ago and 3 years ago, Clay's cancer was misdiagnosed by our community hospital. If we had gone with the diagnosis given us 23 years ago, Clay would have died a slow and extremely painful death (we're not exaggerating).

2. IF I TURN TO MEDICAL HELP, AM I NOT TRUSTING GOD?

Recently, two women asked us if they weren't trusting God if they took medical intervention for their cancers. Sometimes this concern comes from 2 Chronicles 16:12, which reads, "In the thirty-ninth year of his reign Asa was diseased in his feet, and his disease became severe. Yet even in his disease he did not seek the Lord, but sought help from physicians." A prophet previously had rebuked King Asa for waging war without first seeking God's guidance. In response, Asa imprisoned the prophet and cruelly treated the people. The passage above is showing that Asa continued to refuse to seek God even when afflicted with disease. It's not saying that seeking medical help is wrong. Sometimes, God through prophets encouraged particular medical intervention: "Now Isaiah had said, 'Let them take a cake of figs and apply it to the boil, that he may recover'" (Isaiah 38:21).

Consider 1 Timothy 5:23, "No longer drink only water, but use a little wine for the sake of your stomach and your frequent ailments." Timothy had stomach problems and "frequent ailments." Notice that Paul didn't rebuke Timothy for a lack of faith. Paul didn't write, "Next time I see you I will pray for you and God will heal you." Instead, Paul told Timothy to drink "a little wine." That was a medical intervention in that day.

There's nothing sinful about getting medical help for a problem as long as we're also seeking God's help and guidance. As Solomon says in Proverbs 21:31, "The horse is made ready for the day of battle, but the victory belongs to the LORD." We need to get ready for battle, but without the Lord's help it will be to no avail. Similarly, Psalm 127:1 tells us, "Unless the LORD builds the house, those who build it labor in vain. Unless the LORD watches over the city, the watchman stays awake in vain." To build a house or to protect a city, you still need builders and watchmen, but without the Lord's help, their efforts will fail.

Twenty-three years ago, we prayed for healing and guidance over Clay's back pain. The Lord answered by having the surgeon next door tell him to get a CT, and then by having Clay's orthopedic surgeon refer him to a renowned orthopedic oncologist. The Lord used this skilled oncologist to save Clay's life. Sometimes God heals miraculously. Other times He heals through medical care with the wisdom He gives. Both are answers to prayer.

3. IS MEDICALLY RECOMMENDED TREATMENT WORTHWHILE?

One of the biggest questions facing those who need major medical intervention regards whether the intervention is worth it. In other words, will someone's quality of life be so diminished that it would be better to do nothing at all? There's no simple answer to this question.

Everyone facing possible life-changing treatments must get the best advice possible from medical professionals and wise friends. As Solomon writes in Proverbs 24:6, "For by wise guidance you can wage your war, and in abundance of counselors there is victory."[1] You need wisdom to wage your war against whatever threatens your life. Solomon also writes in Proverbs 15:22, "Without counsel plans fail, but with many advisers they succeed." While you're seeking wise counsel, pray fervently for guidance. As Solomon puts it in Proverbs 3:6: "In all your ways acknowledge him, and he will make straight your paths."

4. HOW DO I SUPPORT OTHERS WHO SUFFER?

Many Christians don't know how to respond to those in crisis.[2] Paul in Romans 12:15 says we are to "Rejoice with those who rejoice, weep with those who weep." What this means is that we should meet people where they are emotionally. Is someone okay with where they are in their suffering? Then don't be sadder than they are. Some Christians want to bring others to tears (as when TV interviewers ask questions specifically meant to invoke tears in the interviewee). We shouldn't do that. Now that being said, showing sincere compassion may allow the sufferer to show more emotion and perhaps start crying.

It is when people cry that many Christians don't know what to do. So, what should we do if people start crying?

Listen and let them cry! In other words, don't try to get them to stop. We often want to stop them because we don't know what else to do. The best thing you can do is to let them cry. Simply be there with them. You don't need to come to tears yourself, but show compassion. That's what Paul means when he writes, "Weep with those who weep."

Related to the above, unless you have one within reach, don't offer to go get them a tissue, or anything like that. Now if they appear visibly self-conscious of the fact that they are getting gooey, then offer to get one. Otherwise, let them cry. Offering to go get them a tissue can send the message, "You're getting kind of messy right now; let me help you fix it." Just let people cry. If we know people may be emotional around us, then we have a box of tissues within their reach so that they can get one if they want. I've seen some so upset that they didn't care that their nose was running and makeup was streaking down their cheeks. They were simply glad to be heard by someone who cared.

Let the crying person set the amount of personal space they want. We let people in crisis choose how close they want to be to us by sitting down first and letting them choose how close or far they want to be. Some people will sit across the room; others will sit right next to us.

Don't say, "Don't cry," or "Everything will be okay," or "God is in control," or "It will all work out for good." This kind of comment is mostly for our sake, not theirs, and it delegitimizes their tears. When people cry, it's easy to blab bromides to try to stop the crying. Don't do it—crying is good for people in crises.

Do encourage people to talk about what's upsetting them. If someone gets unexpectedly emotional, ask if they want to talk about it. That will let them decide if they want to get more emotional with you. People need to talk to someone with a listening ear.

Let the tearful person decide how much physical contact they would like. People differ widely on this and respond differently with different people, depending on how safe they feel. This is simple to figure out. If someone is crying, we might reach out to gently and briefly touch them on the shoulder (depending on their body language). If you do that, you will know immediately whether the person you've touched wants more or less contact. Some people will immediately move slightly away. This means no more touching. Others will lean towards you, which means your touch is welcome. Some people have hugged us in that situation. Whatever the case, it's not about you.

You're trying to make the other person feel comfortable. I should add that most men don't want another man to hug or even touch them if they're in tears (that might be different in other cultures).

Ask if there is some way you can help. Give concrete suggestions that you really mean, like offering to bring a meal. (Meals were a great blessing to us when Clay had cancer the first time. We were so overwhelmed, and not having to shop and cook was a relief.) But if you offer to do something—do it. Sadly, we've had people offer to help us and then when we've responded by telling them of a real need they could easily meet, all we received in response were crickets.

If you really want to help someone who has just suffered a major loss, take them a meal (or two). If they attend your church, find out if the church has a ministry that organizes meals for members.

If you realistically have time, tell them that you'd be glad to talk with them more—that you're there for them. But then make sure you are there for them. That gives people hope and makes them feel like they are not alone. As Paul writes in Galatians 6:2, "Bear one another's burdens, and so fulfill the law of Christ."

5. MY DOCTOR SAYS I HAVE ONLY A SHORT TIME TO LIVE. SHOULD I SPEND THAT ENTIRE TIME IN PRAYER AND BIBLE READING?

In some ways, knowing your appointed time is near is a gift allowing you to accomplish what's most important in your life now. Contemplating imminent death is wise: "So teach us to number our days that we may get a heart of wisdom" (Psalm 90:12).

If spending all your remaining time drawing near to God in prayer and study of His Word most appeals to you, by all means do so. We encourage you to spend daily time in prayer and the Bible, but also to do activities you enjoy. Ecclesiastes 5:18 reads, "Behold, what I have seen to be good and fitting is to eat and drink and find enjoyment in all the toil with which one toils under the sun the few days of his life that God has given him, for this is his lot." Likewise, Ecclesiastes 3:12-13 counsels, "I perceived that there is nothing better for them than to be joyful and to do good as long as they live; also that everyone should eat and drink and take pleasure in all his toil—this is God's gift to man."

Here are other worthwhile activities to consider.

Make peace with God. Regularly confess sins and accept God's forgiveness (1 John 1:9). Meditate on the glory that awaits you.

Make peace with others. Romans 12:18 reads, "If possible, so far as it depends on you, be at peace with all men" (NASB1995). Similarly, Jesus says, "If you are offering your gift at the altar and there remember that your brother has something against you, leave your gift there before the altar and go. First be reconciled to your brother, and then come and offer your gift" (Matthew 5:23-24). If any relationships are strained, try to bring peace. If you've wronged anyone, this is your chance to apologize and make things right. Express your love to friends and family.

Honor Christ. When the apostle Paul wrote to the Philippian church from a Roman prison, he didn't know whether the court would execute or free him. He wrote, "It is my eager expectation and hope that I will not be at all ashamed, but that with full courage now as always Christ will be honored in my body, whether by life or by death" (Philippians 1:20). In other words, he hoped to honor Christ courageously whether the outcome was life or death. Pray to honor your Lord during your remaining days.

Remember that death is gain. Paul could honor Christ because living for Christ was his life's purpose and death ended life's suffering. He explained, "For to me to live is Christ, and to die is gain" (Philippians 1:21). Remember that "to die is gain." Paul continued in verse 23, "My desire is to depart and be with Christ, for that is far better." Your earthly suffering will end, and you'll be reunited with loved ones. You'll be in Jesus' presence soon.

Finish fruitful labor. Paul meant to live out his remaining days, however short, in fruitful labor. Philippians 1:22 reads, "If I am to live in the flesh, that means fruitful labor for me." Paul used his imprisonment to share the gospel with prison guards and the officials at his trial. He also wrote letters to churches and church leaders to encourage their spiritual growth. What kind of fruitful labor can you do? With whom can you share Christ? Whom can you encourage? One friend of ours who has ovarian cancer regularly calls a woman in hospice to read psalms to her. Pray for insight into how you might fruitfully labor in your current circumstances.

Wait for the Lord. He is bringing you home to Him. Wait patiently for Him. "Wait for the LORD; be strong, and let your heart take courage; wait for the LORD!" (Psalm 27:14).

6. WHY AM I FACING DEATH AT SO YOUNG AN AGE?

Some face death young; some old. But one of the reasons God brings people out of this world to Himself is to save them from further suffering on earth. Isaiah 57:1-2 reads, "The righteous man perishes, and no one lays it to heart; devout men are taken away, while no one understands. For the righteous man is taken away from calamity; he enters into peace; they rest in their beds who walk in their uprightness."

7. DOESN'T GOD ALWAYS WANT TO HEAL CHRISTIANS?

There's a false doctrine afloat to which some Christians cling, and it is that God always wants to heal on this earth. When I (Clay) was a teenager, I believed and taught that. The trouble with this belief is twofold. First, it isn't taught by Scripture. Second, those who hold to it feel incredibly disillusioned and even angry with God when they get an incurable disease, especially if that incurable disease is terminal. We have talked to many Christians who have felt severely let down by

God when they were diagnosed with a terminal disease. This often results in a crisis of faith. After all, if one clings to the idea that it's always God's will to heal but He doesn't, then that person is going to question God's goodness or even existence because it appears He has not kept His end of the bargain.

But that God always wants to heal on this earth is a false doctrine. As was mentioned above, in 1 Timothy 5:23 Paul tells Timothy, "No longer drink only water, but use a little wine for the sake of your stomach and your frequent ailments." We see that Timothy had stomach problems and "frequent ailments." Notice that Paul doesn't rebuke Timothy for a lack of faith. Paul doesn't write, "Next time I see you I will pray for you and God will heal you." Instead, Paul tells Timothy to drink "a little wine."

In 2 Timothy 4:20, Paul writes, "I left Trophimus sick at Miletus" (NASB). What? Paul didn't heal Trophimus?

Paul writes in Philippians 2:26-27 about Epaphroditus who was "distressed because you heard that he was ill. Indeed he was ill, near to death. But God had mercy on him, and not only on him but on me also, lest I should have sorrow upon sorrow." Notice that Paul doesn't write, "Of course God healed him!" Rather Paul writes that "God had mercy on him." Also, God had mercy upon Paul lest he "should have sorrow upon sorrow." There is nothing in this passage indicating that Paul had an unshakable confidence that God would heal Epaphroditus.

There are other passages, such as Paul's thorn in the flesh (2 Corinthians 12:7-10) that also show it is not always God's will to answer prayers affirmatively. But consider that throughout the ages, the overwhelming majority of Christians have died and will die due to disease (unless one dies by murder or accident), so believing that God always wants to heal will one day be shown to be false.

Final healing comes at the resurrection.

A secular worldview may lie under some Christians' belief that

God must always want to heal; namely, that the greatest good is happiness. As Australian Bible teacher Paul Grimmond writes, "In a world without God, painlessness is the new moral standard. The only great truth is that suffering must be avoided at all costs."[3] As we've shown in this book, God uses suffering for great good. More importantly, this worldview utterly ignores the rewards God promises for faithfulness through suffering.

Our troubles here will seem "light" and "momentary" compared to the "eternal weight of glory" that awaits faithful Christians (2 Corinthians 4:17). When we forget the glorious eternity that awaits, we are in danger of becoming like the Hebrews whose faith faltered when facing persecution (Hebrews 10:32-36; 12:3). Hebrews 12:1 tells them to "lay aside" the "sin which clings so closely." Verse 4 admonishes, "In your struggle against sin you have not yet resisted to the point of shedding your blood." Grimmond writes:

> These people are tottering on the edge of giving up their faith because they are suffering for living for Christ. People are ridiculing them, persecuting them and threatening them with prison. Their external circumstances seem almost unbearable. But where does the author of Hebrews tell us the real issue is? Is it with the evil authorities who have thrown them into prison and confiscated their property? It is not. The real problem lies in their sinful hearts. Have they struggled enough against sin? Have they struggled against sin to the point of shedding blood?
>
> My first reaction to this rebuke is indignation. How pastorally insensitive! Why give these struggling Christians such a slap in the face? Yet here is the wisdom of God. As these people suffer, what really matters? It is whether they will stick with Christ or let him go. And so the great

> struggle of suffering is not particularly with outside powers and forces, but with our stubborn, sinful hearts.[4]

The greatest good is not our happiness on this earth. The greatest good is glorifying the God who gave His Son to free us from sin that we might have an eternity of happiness with Him. The resurrection comes with glorious, immortal bodies. Pain and sorrow end. Eternal joy awaits.

8. WILL EACH PERSON BE GIVEN DIFFERENT REWARDS IN HEAVEN?

There's a lot of confusion and disagreement over whether some Christians will be rewarded more than others. We hold that some Christians will be more rewarded than others, but those greater rewards will be based on humble service, not accomplishment. In 1 Corinthians 3:10, Paul says that he "laid a foundation," which is Jesus Christ, and others are building upon it. He warns, "Let each one take care how he builds upon it." Then Paul says, "Now if anyone builds on the foundation with gold, silver, precious stones, wood, hay, straw—each one's work will become manifest, for the Day will disclose it, because it will be revealed by fire, and the fire will test what sort of work each one has done" (verses 12-13). In other words, all our work here will be examined at the judgment. Paul continues, "If the work that anyone has built on the foundation survives, he will receive a reward. If anyone's work is burned up, he will suffer loss, though he himself will be saved, but only as through fire" (verses 14-15). Notice that if a Christian's work "survives, he will receive a reward." But Paul says that some Christians' work of "wood, hay, straw" will be "burned up." But thankfully, Paul then quickly adds that the Christian "himself will be saved, but only as through fire." There it is. We aren't saved by works, but those who honor God through difficulties, through suffering, will be rewarded more than careless builders. This encourages us because we know that some of our work fits into the "wood, hay, straw" category, and that's embarrassing. About this passage Gordon Fee writes, "Thus as surely as there is final judgment, there are also 'reward' and 'loss.' What is *not* known, either from this passage or elsewhere, is the nature of the reward."[5]

In the parable of the ten minas in Luke 19, Jesus told of a nobleman who went away to receive a kingdom and then return. Prior to leaving, he gave each of his ten servants a mina (one mina was worth about four months' wages) and encouraged them to "engage in business until I come" (verse 13). He wanted them to make a profit. After receiving his kingdom, the nobleman returned and demanded an accounting of his servants. Jesus says in verses 16-19: "The first came before him, saying, 'Lord, your mina has made ten minas more.' And he said to him, 'Well done, good servant! Because you have been faithful in a very little, you shall have authority over ten cities.' And the second came, saying, 'Lord, your mina has made five minas.' And he said to him, 'And you are to be over five cities.' "

Then another servant came, but he had done nothing with the mina except set it in a safe place. The nobleman's response to him was to take his mina away and give it to the man who had ten minas (verse 24). It's clear in this parable that those who are faithful will be rewarded with more authority than those who are less faithful.

Similarly, Paul says in 1 Corinthians 4:5: "Therefore do not pronounce judgment before the time, before the Lord comes, who will bring to light the things now hidden in darkness and will disclose the purposes of the heart. Then each one will receive his commendation from God." Notice that motives play a huge part in how people are commended. If our motives are selfish, if we're looking for self-aggrandizement, money, or human recognition, then regardless of what ministry we might have accomplished, at the judgment there may be no reward.

Paul is clear about that in 1 Corinthians 13:1-3:

> If I speak in the tongues of men and of angels, but have not love, I am a noisy gong or a clanging cymbal. And if I have prophetic powers, and understand all mysteries and all knowledge, and if I have all faith, so as to remove mountains, but have not love, I am nothing. If I give away all I have, and if I deliver up my body to be burned, but have not love, I gain nothing.

In other words, you can write many books and speak to thousands, or serve nonstop in soup kitchens, and so on, but if you did it from the wrong motives—if it wasn't done out of love—there is no reward. We're paid in full. Therefore, a Christian woman working in a memory care facility may receive greater commendation from God than the Christian author who has spoken to thousands. What we accomplish counts less than the motive by which we accomplish it.

We want to emphasize that the size of one's ministry isn't the point. Many Christians think that those who've had the largest public ministries will receive the most rewards in heaven. Few things could be further from the truth. In Luke 16:10, Jesus says, "The one who is faithful in a very little thing is also faithful in much; and the one who is unrighteous in a very little thing is also unrighteous in much" (NASB). In other words, if you honor God in things the world may consider insignificant, then you will honor God when you are given what the Lord considers significant things.

If it's your turn to bring refreshments to a church Bible study, do it well. Taking good care of an elderly or a disabled person is no less honorable in our Lord's eyes than writing a Christian bestseller. Besides, bestselling authors receive emotional and financial rewards now. People praise their books, ministries ask them to speak, and they can be well paid. Contrast that with the woman who honorably cares for a sick neighbor or a disabled child—there can be little or no earthly reward. But, says Jesus, if you are faithful in what the world considers a "little thing," then you will also be faithful in "much." Now, we're not saying that the successful Christian author will receive more or less reward than the person who lovingly cares for a sick neighbor or disabled child; we're simply saying that we don't know to what extent each will be rewarded. Rewards will be based on faithfulness and on our motives.

Jesus says something similar in Matthew 18:1-4: "At that time the disciples came to Jesus, saying, 'Who is the greatest in the kingdom of heaven?' And calling to him a child, he put him in the midst of them and said, 'Truly, I say to you, unless you turn and become like children, you will never enter the kingdom of heaven. Whoever humbles himself like this child is the greatest in the kingdom of heaven.'" Who will be greatest? The most humble! Not the most famous or respected. Likewise, Jesus says in Matthew 23:11-12, "The greatest among you shall be your servant. Whoever exalts himself will be humbled, and whoever humbles himself will be exalted."

Luke 22 has similar teaching. The disciples argued about who would be "regarded as the greatest. And he said to them, 'The kings of the Gentiles exercise lordship over them'" (verses 24-25). Then says Jesus, "But not so with you. Rather, let the greatest among you become as the youngest, and the leader as one who serves. For who is the greater, one who reclines at table or one who serves? Is it not the one who reclines at table? But I am among you as the one who serves" (verses 26-27). Notice that Jesus doesn't say, "Hey, come on guys, no one is going to be greater than anyone else. Everyone will be equal in every way." Also, notice that in the kingdom, those who are considered greatest will be the "one who serves" and they won't "exercise lordship" over others. Serving is a type of suffering and Jesus is aptly called the Suffering Servant.

Similarly, in Matthew 20:21, a mother asks Jesus to appoint her sons, James and John, "to sit, one at your right hand and one at your left, in your kingdom." In verse 23, Jesus replies, "To sit at my right hand and at my left is not mine to grant, but it is for those for whom it has been prepared by my Father." Notice that Jesus doesn't say, "Come on, everyone, there won't be someone permanently seated at My right hand and at My left hand. You will all take turns. You'll all get an equal chance." The passage goes on: "And when the ten heard it, they were indignant at the two brothers" (verse 24). But, in verses 25-28, Jesus says, "You know that the rulers of the Gentiles lord it over them, and their great ones exercise authority over them. It shall not be so among you. But whoever would be great among you must be your servant, and whoever would be first among you must be your slave, even as the Son of Man came not to be served but to serve, and to give his life as a ransom for many." There it is again, the "first among [us] must be your slave." Jesus came to suffer on the cross. Jesus is saying that those who rule won't lord it over us, but if someone is going to be greatest, then he will be the greatest servant.

No one needs to be concerned about there being different rewards or levels of reward. We suspect that the levels of rewards will be about levels of responsibility. Being put in charge over "cities" is about responsibility. Being given more "talents" to invest isn't the same as someone being given a mansion on beachfront property while the rest of us live in tents on the street; it too is about being given responsibility. Jesus, the King of kings and the Lord of lords has the most responsibility of anyone but humbled Himself, "took on the form of a servant," washed His disciples' feet, and allowed Himself to be spit on, mocked, struck, scourged, and crucified for the sake of those who had less responsibility.

Those who will be rewarded with the most responsibility and acclaim will be those who are most like Jesus. He suffered in His service to others. At the judgment we will all see that, and so we will be pleased to serve with them. The world judges success by how famous or influential a person has become, but the Lord judges success by our motives while we serve Him in spite of suffering. Again, Romans

8:16-17 tells us: "The Spirit himself bears witness with our spirit that we are children of God, and if children, then heirs—heirs of God and fellow heirs with Christ, provided we suffer with him in order that we may also be glorified with him." Our eternal glory and recognition come by our honoring God through suffering!

NOTES

PREFACE

1. This is adapted from a joke variously attributed to Will Rogers or Jack Handy, but some sites, such as Carnegie-Mellon University, list no attribution, https://www.cs.cmu.edu/afs/cs/usr/will/www/Quotes.html, accessed May 31, 2023.

INTRODUCTION: PREPARING TO CONQUER

1. C.S. Lewis, *The Problem of Pain* (New York: Macmillan, 1953), 132.
2. The paragraph that follows was adapted from Clay's book, *Immortal: How the Fear of Death Drives Us and What We Can Do About It* (Eugene, OR: Harvest House, 2020), 206.
3. "Glorious," Merriam-Webster's Dictionary, https://www.merriam-webster.com/dictionary/glorious, accessed December 7, 2024.
4. The word "spring" is to be preferred over "because." As G.K. Beale put it: "The more precise nuance here is that love 'spring[s] from' (NIV) or arises from hope." G.K. Beale, *Colossians and Philemon*, Baker Exegetical Commentary on the New Testament (Grand Rapids, MI: Baker, 2019), 37.
5. Richard R. Melick, *Philippians, Colossians, Philemon*, The New American Commentary (Nashville, TN: Broadman and Holman, 1991), 195. As Melick puts it, "Paul believed that the hope offered in Christ inspires assurance and, as a result, produces spiritual fruit. The basis of believing Christ (faith) and serving others (love) is that this world is not the end. There is an afterlife where the deeds done here will be evaluated and rewarded. Christians have an understanding of the rewards and blessings of heaven." Ibid., 197.
6. Although Martin Luther said something similar, this wording is from John Calvin, *Antidote to the Council of Trent* (1547), as quoted in Steve Bauer, "Is Luther really the originator of 'We are saved by faith alone, but the faith that saves is never alone'?," August 5, 2015, StackExchange, https://christianity.stackexchange.com/questions/42366/is-luther-really-the-originator-of-we-are-saved-by-faith-alone-but-the-faith-t, accessed November 17, 2020.
7. Martin Luther, *95 Theses*, as quoted in Sam Logan, "What Did Martin Luther Actually Say in His 95 Theses?," World Reformed Fellowship, July 29, 2017, https://wrf.global/blog/blog-3/what-did-martin-luther-actually-say-his-95-theses, accessed November 17, 2020.

8. The Bible does not support the notion of "non-lordship" salvation (that a person can have Jesus only as Savior and not Lord and so does not need to change their lives in any way). Also, we reject the notion that praying the sinner's prayer, of itself, has any salvific power. Clay has posted on this: https://clayjones.net/2010/06/the-sinners-prayer-never-saved-anyone/. One who has come to a saving faith will certainly produce, as Luther wrote in thesis 3, "various outward mortifications of the flesh."

9. If you'd like to learn more about prayer, two of Jean's books offer guidance. *Discovering Joy in Philippians* (Harvest House, 2019) shows how to pray meditatively while reading the Bible and how to pray Paul's prayers in Philippians. *Discovering Hope in the Psalms* (Harvest House, 2017) provides step-by-step instructions on writing and praying psalms.

10. C.S. Lewis, *The Screwtape Letters* (New York: Macmillan, 1961), 46.

11. Clay Jones, *Why Does God Allow Evil?: Compelling Answers for Life's Toughest Questions* (Eugene, OR: Harvest House, 2017), 112.

12. Lewis, *Screwtape Letters*, 46.

13. Lewis, *Screwtape Letters*, 47.

14. For more on this see Clay's post: "Lusting after God and His Kingdom," clayjones.net, June 2011, https://clayjones.net/2011/06/lusting-after-god-and-his-kingdom/, accessed January 15, 2025.

15. In Revelation 2:10-11, Jesus says to the Christians at Smyrna, "Be faithful unto death, and I will give you the crown of life. He who has an ear, let him hear what the Spirit says to the churches. The one who conquers will not be hurt by the second death." This worries some Christians because that could be misunderstood as meaning that Christians must give their lives for the gospel to be saved. But, although Jesus proclaims different blessings to each of the seven churches, all of the blessings that He mentions apply to all of the overcomers. G.K. Beale makes an important point regarding Revelation 3:5: "The one who conquers will be clothed thus in white garments, and I will never blot his name out of the book of life. I will confess his name before my Father and before his angels." Beale continues, "Verse 5 shows that the promise to the conqueror cannot be limited to martyrs but includes all Christians, since it would be unthinkable that the names of all true believers would not be found in the 'the book of life.' The same is also the case with Christ's confession of names before the Father." G.K. Beale, *The Book of Revelation*, New International Greek Testament Commentary (Grand Rapids, MI: Eerdmans, 1999), 281.

16. For more on this, see Clay's blog entitled, "The Lord Made Orgasms Possible," clayjones.net, https://clayjones.net/2022/01/the-lord-made-orgasms-possible/, accessed January 15, 2025.

CHAPTER 1—TRUTHS ABOUT VICTORY IN SUFFERING

1. Adapted from Jean E. Jones, "The Journey of Childlessness," *Today's Christian Woman*, April 2010, https://www.todayschristianwoman.com/articles/2010/april/journeychildlessness.html, accessed August 20, 2024.

2. William Wright, *All the Pain Money Can Buy: The Life of Christina Onassis* (New York: Simon and Shuster, 1991), 200.

3. G.K. Beale, *The Book of Revelation*, New International Greek Testament Commentary (Grand Rapids, MI: Eerdmans, 1999), 1057.

4. Paige Patterson in his commentary on Revelation writes, "A more literal rendering is found in the Authorized Version, 'I wept much,' which seems to indicate not only extended weeping

but also the nuance of this word as focusing on the loud wailing of profound bitterness. This must have gone on for a while, for the emphasis is on the continuation of the weeping." Paige Patterson, *Revelation*, ed. E. Ray Clendenen, The New American Commentary (Nashville, TN: Broadman and Holman, 2012), 163.

5. Revelation 5:6, NIV but with Beale's clarification. Beale explains, "He conquered death by being raised from the dead. But the present victorious effect of the Lamb's overcoming resides not only in the fact that the Lamb continues to 'stand' but also in the fact that it continues to exist as a *slaughtered* Lamb. The perfect participle…('having been slain') expresses an abiding condition as a result of the past act of being slain…

   …Christ as a Lion overcame by being slaughtered as a Lamb…The translation 'as *though* slain' is unnecessary and misleading, as if the Lamb only looked slain but was not; 'as slain' is best." Beale, *Revelation*, 352.

6. The word *slain* can equally be translated as "slaughtered" (NASB). In this context John probably has the Passover lamb in view. Beale writes, "The slain Lamb thus represents the image of a conqueror who was mortally wounded while defeating an enemy. Christ's death, the end-time sacrifice of the messianic Lamb, becomes interpreted as a sacrifice that not only redeems but also conquers." Beale, *Revelation*, 351.

7. Beale, *Revelation*, 352. Emphasis original.

8. I write "usually" because in some passages, all translations may use a different English word.

9. Corrie ten Boom; Elizabeth Sherrill; John Sherrill, *The Hiding Place* (Grand Rapids, MI: Baker, 1971), 206, Kindle. Ellipsis in the original.

10. "Tribulation," Vocabulary.com, https://www.vocabulary.com/dictionary/tribulation, accessed May 10, 2025.

11. "Distress," Merriam-Webster's Dictionary, https://www.merriam-webster.com/dictionary/distress, accessed January 13, 2025.

12. Adam Goldman and Greg Miller, "Leader of Islamic State took American hostage as sexual slave," *Washington Post*, August 14, 2015, https://www.washingtonpost.com/world/national-security/leader-of-islamic-state-raped-american-hostage/2015/08/14/266b6bf4-42c1-11e5-846d-02792f854297_story.html, accessed January 17, 2025. The *Washington Post* article goes on to say, "A recent issue of the English-language magazine published by the Islamic State described the taking of sex slaves as religiously justified. The article—titled 'Slave girls or prostitutes?'—endorsed the practice, saying sex slaves are 'lawful for the one who ends up possessing them even without pronouncement of divorce by their [non-Muslim] husbands.'" See also, "US hostage Kayla Mueller 'killed by IS', say ex-slaves," *BBC*, September 10, 2015, https://www.bbc.com/news/world-middle-east-34205911, accessed January 18, 2025.

13. See Sean McDowell, *The Fate of the Apostles: Examining the Martyrdom Accounts of the Closest Followers of Jesus* (Burlington, VT: Ashgate, 2015), 111-114.

14. D.A. Carson, *The Gospel According to John*, Pillar New Testament Commentary (Grand Rapids, MI: Eerdmans, 1991), 579.

15. Mary Beard, *The Roman Triumph* (Cambridge, MA: Harvard, 2007), 1.

16. Beard, *The Roman Triumph*, 1.

17. Beard, *The Roman Triumph*, 4.

18. Of course, we are not suggesting that the Christian can't take a vacation or enjoy times of leisure, but our Lord will not let that be the majority of our existence.

19. David E. Garland, *2 Corinthians*, The New American Commentary (Nashville, TN: Broadman and Holman, 1999), 147.
20. "US hostage Kayla Mueller 'killed by IS', say ex-slaves," *BBC*, September 10, 2015, https://www.bbc.com/news/world-middle-east-34205911, accessed January 18, 2025.
21. Desmond Busteed, "Obama confirms death of Christian hostage," *Premier Christian News*, February 10, 2015, https://premierchristian.news/en/news/article/obama-confirms-death-of-christian-hostage?recommid=6a13ce4a70c6242c181a6158fa41f8e9, accessed January 17, 2025. Emphasis authors'.
22. Amy Goodman, "Former ISIS Hostage Nicolas Hénin: Welcoming Refugees is the Best Strategy Against ISIS," *Democracy Now*, January 1, 2016, https://www.democracynow.org/2016/1/1/former_isis_hostage_nicolas_henin_welcoming, accessed January 18, 2025.
23. Brian Ross, "The Girl Left Behind: Kayla Mueller Part 2: Former ISIS Hostages Speak Out," *Brian Ross Investigates 20/20 ABC News*, August 2016, https://abcnews.go.com/International/fullpage/brian-ross-investigates-kayla-mueller-girl-left-41600838, accessed January 18, 2025. See also, Desmond Busteed, "Islamic State leader 'raped' US Christian hostage Kayla Mueller," *Premier Christian News*, August, 15 2015, https://premierchristian.news/en/news/article/islamic-state-leader-raped-us-christian-hostage-kayla-mueller, accessed January 15, 2025.
24. Brian Ross, "The Girl Left Behind: Kayla Mueller Part 5: Kayla's Sacrifice Allows ISIS Slave to Escape," *Brian Ross Investigates 20/20 ABC News*, August 2016, https://abcnews.go.com/International/fullpage/brian-ross-investigates-kayla-mueller-girl-left-41600838, accessed January 18, 2025.
25. Richard Wurmbrand, *Tortured for Christ* (Bartlesville, OK: Living Sacrifice, 1967), 153, Kindle.
26. This is adapted from Clay's book, *Why Does God Allow Evil?: Compelling Answers for Life's Toughest Questions* (Eugene, OR: Harvest House, 2017), 198-200.

CHAPTER 2—TRUTH 1: GOD LOVES US

1. Jane Austen, *Pride and Prejudice* (New York: Walter J. Black, 1941), 179-198.
2. Evans also writes, "It doesn't make sense to me that a God whose defining characteristic is supposed to be love would present Himself to His creation in a way that looks nothing like our understanding of love. If love can look like abuse…everything is relativized! Our moral compass is rendered totally unreliable." Rachel Held Evans, "I would fail Abraham's test (and I bet you would too)," https://rachelheldevans.com/blog/fail-abraham-test, accessed August 13, 2024. For the first of Jean's five-part response, see "Was Abraham Wrong? Answering Rachel Held Evans, Part 1," https://www.jeanejones.net/2015/10/was-abraham-wrong-answering-rachel-held-evans-part-1/, accessed August 16, 2024.
3. Human sacrifices found in Ur date prior to and during the age in which Abraham lived. See Laerke Recht, "Human sacrifice in the ancient Near East," Trinity College Dublin Journal of Postgraduate Research (Dublin: Brunswick Press, 2010), 9:171.
4. Paul Copan, *Is God a Moral Monster?: Making Sense of the Old Testament God* (Grand Rapids, MI: Baker, 2011), 47.
5. Timothy George, *Galatians*, The New American Commentary (Nashville, TN: Broadman and Holman, 1994), 225, Logos.
6. Abraham is called a prophet in Genesis 20:7. Isaac received visions and divine revelations in 26:1-4, 24. Psalm 105:9, 15 calls Abraham and Isaac "anointed ones" and "prophets."

7. Isaiah 8:18: "Behold, I and the children whom the LORD has given me are signs and portents in Israel from the LORD of hosts." A *portent* is a sign or warning that something, especially something momentous or calamitous, is likely to happen.

8. The story of Abraham binding Isaac is in Genesis 22; the prior chapter (21) brings Isaac to adolescence and in the following chapter (23) he is 37. The ESV translates the Hebrew word *na'ar* as "boy" in Genesis 22:5 and 12 but elsewhere translates it "young man." The word is used of the trained men who went with Abraham to rescue Lot (Genesis 14:24); of the men who attempted to rape angels (Genesis 19:4); of Joseph at age 28 (Genesis 41:12); of the spies whom Rahab hid (Joshua 6:23); of trained soldiers (2 Samuel 2:14); and of Absalom when he tried to overthrow David's throne (2 Samuel 18:32).

9. D.A. Carson lecture in Hermeneutics and Homiletics, Doctor of Ministry program, Trinity Evangelical Divinity School, January 2002.

10. Regarding "For this reason the Father loves me," D.A. Carson explains: "It is not that the Father withholds his love until Jesus agrees to give up his life on the cross and rise again. Rather, the love of the Father for the Son is eternally linked with the unqualified obedience of the Son to the Father, his utter dependence upon him, culminating in the greatest act of obedience now just before him: willingness to bear the shame and ignominy of Golgotha, the isolation and rejection of death, the sin and curse reserved for the Lamb of God." D.A. Carson, *The Gospel According to John*, Pillar New Testament Commentary (Grand Rapids, MI: Eerdmans, 1991), 388.

11. D.A. Carson, *Matthew*, The Expositor's Bible Commentary (Grand Rapids, MI: Zondervan, 2010), 1199, Kindle. Of course, Jesus wasn't trying to provide the precise number of angels at His disposal. Jesus was simply saying that an overwhelming force was instantly available to Him any time He asked.

12. Millard Erickson, *Christian Theology* (Grand Rapids, MI: Baker, 1996), 735-736.

13. Jesus is called "King of kings" and "Lord of lords" in Revelation 17:14 and 19:16.

14. William D. Edwards, MD; Wesley J. Gabel, MDiv; Floyd E. Hosmer, MS, AMI, "On the Physical Death of Jesus Christ," *Journal of the American Medical Association*, March 21, 1986, v. 255, n.11, 1456, https://people.bethel.edu/~pferris/ot103/Jesus_Crucifixion.pdf, accessed September 6, 2024.

15. The *fustigatio* was for light offences. Often, the prisoner was then released with a warning, which is what Pilate offered to do. The harsh *flagellatio* was for serious offences. See D.A. Carson, *The Gospel According to John*, Pillar New Testament Commentary (Grand Rapids, MI: Eerdmans, 1991), 597.

16. The horrible *verberatio* accompanied crucifixion. Carson, *The Gospel According to John*, 597.

17. Although the passage doesn't specifically say that Jesus was stripped, they always stripped people prior to scourging them.

18. Edwards, "On the Physical Death of Jesus Christ," 1457.

19. Craig Blomberg, *Matthew*, The New American Commentary (Nashville, TN: Broadman and Holman, 1992), 417.

20. At our church's 2025 Easter service, a fellow of 55–60 years of age that I (Clay) had never met before told Jean and me that a sermon where I gave a graphic explanation of Jesus' nakedness on the cross had changed his life. He said he had never once even considered the possibility. He said he now tells others that this is part of what Jesus endured.

21. Edwards, "On the Physical Death of Jesus Christ," 1461.

22. Edwards, "On the Physical Death of Jesus Christ," 1459.

23. Carson, *Matthew*, 1265.

24. Douglass Moo, *Old Testament in the Gospel Passion Narratives* (Sheffield: Almond, 1983), 274 as quoted by Carson, *Matthew*, 1265. Carson writes: "If we ask in what ontological sense the Father and the Son are here divided, the answer must be that we do not know because we are not told. If we ask for what purpose they are divided, the ultimate answer must be tied in with Gethsemane, the Last Supper, passion passages such as 1:21; 20:28 (see also 26:26-29, 39-44), and the theological interpretation articulated by Paul (e.g., Ro 3:21-26)." Carson, *Matthew*, 1265.

25. Blomberg, *Matthew*, 419.

26. Carson, *Matthew*, 1266-1267.

CHAPTER 3—TRUTH 2: EVERYONE IS GOING TO GO THROUGH THIS

1. At least that's true in the Western world. Those in poorer countries may not have easy access to doctors.

2. "Couple Follows Their Hearts; Billions Dead," *The Babylon Bee*, June 9, 2016, https://babylonbee.com/news/couple-follows-hearts-billions-dead, accessed August 7, 2024.

3. Although the early church fathers unanimously believed these verses *also* referred to Satan, many commentators today say these passages refer only to earthly kings because Satan wouldn't have been the earthly author's intent. But this hermeneutic is being questioned (e.g., Vern S. Poythress, "Dispensing with Merely Human Meaning: Gains and Losses from Focusing on the Human Author, Illustrated by Zephaniah 1:2-3," *JETS*, 27, No 3 [September 2014], 501-512), and some recent commentators are again applying these passages to Satan (e.g., Lamar Eugene Cooper, *Ezekiel*, The New American Commentary [Nashville, TN: Broadman and Holman, 1994]). After all, Satan is sometimes addressed through the creature he is influencing (Genesis 3:14-15; Matthew 16:23). Cooper explains, "The sinister character of the mastermind behind God's enemies is not always recognized. The real motivating force behind the king of Tyre was the adversary, the satan, who opposed God and his people from the beginning (28:6-19)." Cooper, *Ezekiel*, 269.

4. Lamar Cooper is right: "Who, then, was the person whose character was like the king of Tyre that fulfilled the elements of vv. 12-17? The serpent was known for his craftiness (Gen 3:1), his deceit, and his anti-God attitude (3:4), leading humanity to sin (3:6-7). Elsewhere he is presented as a deceiver (Rev 12:9; 20:2), an instigator of evil (John 13:2, 27), one who seeks worship as a god (Luke 4:6-8; 2 Thess 2:3-4), and one who seeks to get others to renounce God (Job 2:4-5). He appears as an angel of God (2 Cor 11:14) and as the father of lies and violence (John 8:44), distorts Scripture (Matt 4:6), opposes believers (2 Cor 2:11), and finally is judged (Matt 25:41; Rev 19:20-21; 20:13-15). Therefore the conclusion that the figure behind the poetic symbol is the serpent (also known as the adversary, the devil, Satan; Rev 12:9) is a logical one." Cooper, *Ezekiel*, 268.

5. See also Zechariah 3:1 and Job chapters 1 and 2.

6. Clay Jones, *Why Does God Allow Evil?: Compelling Answers for Life's Toughest Questions* (Eugene, OR: Harvest House, 2017).

7. G.K. Beale, *The Book of Revelation*, New International Greek Testament Commentary (Grand Rapids, MI: Eerdmans, 1999), 659.

8. Douglas J. Moo, *The Letter of James*, Pillar New Testament Commentary (Grand Rapids, MI: Eerdmans, 2000), 70.
9. For an in-depth look at Psalms 42–43 and step-by-step instructions on how to write a prayer based on them, see Jean's *Discovering Hope in the Psalms* (Harvest House, 2017).
10. "The Four Spiritual Laws," Cru, https://www.cru.org/content/movementlife/ph/en/how-to-know-god/would-you-like-to-know-god-personally1.html, accessed January 27, 2025.
11. "Military camaraderie is a unique bond that transcends time, duty, and service. It's a connection that's often hard to describe yet so palpable for those who've experienced it. Whether on the front lines or during times of peace, the sense of belonging and mutual respect within the military community is unparalleled." "Celebrating Military Camaraderie: What to Expect at MCON," *Military Times*, https://www.militarytimes.com/native/mcon/2023/10/16/celebrating-military-camaraderie-what-to-expect-at-mcon/, accessed January 15, 2025.
12. John 17:22-23: "The glory that you have given me I have given to them, that they may be one even as we are one, I in them and you in me."
13. P.T. O'Brien, *The Letter to the Ephesians* (Grand Rapids, MI: Eerdmans, 1999), 173.
14. Jean's book, *Discovering Joy in Philippians* (Harvest House, 2019), walks readers through rejoicing in blessings and hardships.

CHAPTER 4—TRUTH 3, PART 1: GOD WILL WORK EVERYTHING OUT FOR OUR GOOD

1. I quoted verses like John 1:12; 3:16; 5:24; Romans 10:9 and a host of others—I quickly memorized them.
2. "What Is the Unpardonable Sin?", *Christian Research Journal*, June 21, 2013, https://www.equip.org/articles/what-is-the-unpardonable-sin-2a/, accessed January 25, 2025.
3. Pseudonym.
4. See 1 Corinthians 13:7 and Luke 6:43-45.
5. I'm not going to mention the issue that I wasn't sure about because it would distract from the point of this account.
6. See also Colossians 3:1-4.
7. Our confidence that Christianity is objectively true is based on the historical fact that Jesus was raised from the dead.
8. A.W. Tozer, *The Root of the Righteous* (Chicago, IL: Moody, 2015), 165, Kindle.
9. C.H. Spurgeon, "The Minister in These Times," *An All-Round Ministry* (Edinburgh, UK: Banner of Truth, 2000), 384. Italics in the original.
10. One of these was slightly edited for grammar. All of these appear on Clay's Facebook page.
11. "No single word translates *epieikes* well, and commentators consistently insist that the word contains an element of selflessness. The gentle person does not insist on his rights. 'It is that considerate courtesy and respect for the integrity of others which prompts a man not to be for ever standing on his rights; and it is preeminently the character of Jesus (2 Cor 10:1).' The word occurs in Paul's writing as a characteristic of Christian leaders (1 Tim 3:3, of bishops; Titus 3:2)." Richard R. Melick, *Philippians, Colossians, Philemon*, New American Commentary (Nashville, TN: Broadman and Holman, 1991), 149.

12. In AD 93–94, Josephus wrote, "Festus was now dead, and Albinus was but upon the road; so he assembled the Sanhedrim of judges, and brought before them the brother of Jesus, who was called Christ, whose name was James, and some others; and when he had formed an accusation against them as breakers of the law, he delivered them to be stoned." Josephus, *The Antiquities of the Jews*, 20.200, Flavius Josephus, *The Works of Flavius Josephus*, William Whiston, trans. (Worcester, MA: 1895), https://lexundria.com/j_aj/20.200/wst, accessed October 18, 2024.

CHAPTER 5—TRUTH 3, PART 2: GOD WILL WORK SUFFERING OUT FOR OUR GOOD

1. That we Christians will remember each other and what we've done in this life is a major Christian hope. Revelation 14:13: "And I heard a voice from heaven saying, 'Write this: Blessed are the dead who die in the Lord from now on.' 'Blessed indeed,' says the Spirit, 'that they may rest from their labors, for their deeds follow them!'" Notice that our deeds will follow us into heaven. Second Corinthians 1:14: "On the day of our Lord Jesus you will boast of us as we will boast of you." Murray Harris writes, "Paul is hopeful that the Corinthians will soon come to recognize that there are already totally adequate reasons for them to feel proud of him—such as their awareness of his devoted spiritual fatherhood (cf. 1 Cor. 4: 14-15) or their knowledge of his skilled service as a master builder (cf. 1 Cor. 3: 9-10). He reverts to this theme in 5:11-12 where he expresses the hope that his converts at Corinth will reach a proper understanding of his apostolic status and conduct: 'What we are is plain to God, and I hope it is also plain to your conscience…we are giving you cause for pride in us.'" Harris, Murray J. *The Second Epistle to the Corinthians*, New International Greek Testament Commentary (Grand Rapids, MI: Eerdmans, 2005), s.v., "1:13b-14," Kindle. First Thessalonians 2:19-20: "For what is our hope or joy or crown of boasting before our Lord Jesus at his coming? Is it not you? For you are our glory and joy." About this passage D. Michael Martin writes, "At the time of judgment when all would be laid bare, Paul aspired to hear his Lord proclaim, 'Well done' (cf. 1 Cor 4:1-5). Such an aspiration is not pride or arrogance. It is the desire to be judged a good steward by God." D. Michael Martin, *1, 2 Thessalonians*, The New American Commentary (Nashville, TN: Broadman and Holman, 1995), 99. When it comes to Paul boasting in heaven about his accomplishments, we suspect that will be no different than in the parables of the talents (Matthew 25:14-29) and the parable of the minas (Luke 19:11-27). In Luke 19:16-17, the first servant "came before him, saying, 'Lord, your mina has made ten minas more.' And he said to him, 'Well done, good servant! Because you have been faithful in a very little, you shall have authority over ten cities.'"
2. This is also mentioned in Galatians 3:6-7; Romans 4:3-24; and James 2:23.
3. Expositors aren't sure as to what affliction Paul was referring. We suspect a reason that the Lord didn't have Paul specify exactly what he suffered is so that people who suffer in different ways can relate.
4. As Douglas Moo puts it, "'Endurance,' in turn, will, if our attitude is right, produce a 'tested character.' As a result of this tested character, finally, the Christian who responds to suffering with the proper attitude will find, at the end of the line, that hope has been strengthened. Sufferings, rather than threatening or weakening our hope, as we might expect to be the case, will, instead, increase our certainty in that hope." Douglas Moo, *The Epistle to the Romans*, New International Commentary on the New Testament (Grand Rapids, MI: Eerdmans, 1996), 303.
5. See also Deuteronomy 6:10-12; 15:15; 16:2, 12; 24:18, 22.
6. Jordan Peterson says that many people, including his wife, think in pictures, while he thinks primarily in words. Jordan Peterson, "Thinking in Words or Images," *Rational Minds,* August 15, 2022, https://www.youtube.com/watch?v=aqtzkzQpSdY, accessed November 12, 2024. We

are not suggesting that this is what the judgment will be like but rather that this symbolizes how attitudes toward suffering would change if we grasped the Bible's teaching.

7. Those whose bodies have died are currently the "spirits of the righteous made perfect" (Hebrews 12:23). They no longer sin and won't display jealousy.

8. Murray J. Harris writes that in the Old Testament glory "refers principally to the visible manifestation of God's nature, presence, and power." Harris, *Second Corinthians,* s.v., "4:18," Kindle.

9. Harris, *Second Corinthians,* s. v., "4:7," Kindle.

10. NASB: "light affliction is *producing* for us an eternal weight of glory." NIV: "are *achieving* for us an eternal glory."

    David E. Garland: "The passive voice, κατεργάζεται ἡμῖν ('are achieving for us, NIV'), points to God as the agent (see Phil 2:12-13). The thought would parallel Rom 8:28, 'We know that all things work together for good for those who love God, who are called according to his purpose' (NRSV). The 'all things' refer to the sufferings of those who love God (Rom 8:18, 35-39; and 5:3-4). The 'good' refers to their ultimate salvation, not simply good things happening in their lives. Paul affirms in Romans that nothing can really harm those who give their lives to God, but even grievous things serve to help them on their way to salvation, confirming their faith and drawing them closer to God." David E. Garland, *2 Corinthians,* The New American Commentary (Nashville, TN: Broadman and Holman, 1999), s.v., 244, fn 261, Logos.

    Murray Harris writes, "In the divine economy, affliction actually generates glory...While there is a correspondence between the" suffering and glory, "there is no precise proportionality, for the production of the glory operates 'to an utterly incomparable degree.' But, with that said, there must be some unequal correspondence, so that not only does affliction produce glory, but also, the greater the affliction, the greater the glory. So then, Paul's point in v. 17 is this: when compared with the glory that was accumulating 'beyond all measure and proportion,' the suffering he was undergoing in the service of Christ appeared both insignificant and momentary. The suffering was real, not imaginary (cf. vv. 8-11), and if it were viewed" through flesh "with a purely human assessment, it would seem burdensome and prolonged, but when viewed...in the light of eternity, the suffering took on the opposite hue—it seemed slight and temporary. The eye of faith creates a new perspective." Harris, *Second Corinthians,* s.v., "4:17," Kindle.

11. Harris, *Second Corinthians,* s.v., "4:17," Kindle.

12. We should not use 2 Corinthians 5:1 to draw conclusions about the intermediate state and related issues. David E. Garland puts it well: "Gillman is correct in his analysis of Paul's statements in 1 Corinthians 15 and 2 Corinthians 5: 'It would be going too far...to press, as many do, both passages for systematic answers to such questions as *when* the resurrection body is received (death or Parousia?), *what* the nature of the intermediates state is, or *how* the transformation of the earthly body takes place.' Paul did not write this passage to answer questions we might have about the when, what, or how; he only intends to affirm his confidence in the Christian's transformation in the life after death." Garland, *2 Corinthians,* 250.

CHAPTER 6—TRUTH 4: MANY HAVE HONORED GOD THROUGH HARSHER SUFFERING THAN WE HAVE

1. Many Christians have been imprisoned while awaiting torturous executions.

2. We are not suggesting that those struggling to understand God's justice shouldn't seek answers from mature believers—they should! What we're warning against is grumbling that God isn't good for allowing the wicked to succeed for a time. When mature Christians complain about God's goodness, they stumble young Christians.

3. For an in-depth look at Asaph's journey from bitterness and confusion to thankfulness, see Jean's book, *Discovering Hope in the Psalms* (Harvest House, 2017).
4. We aren't talking about complaining about pain or suffering in general but rather complaining against God.
5. Joni Eareckson Tada, "Joni Eareckson Tada Shares Her Story on Larry King Live: From Paralysis to Faith," *Larry King Live*, August 3, 2004, https://transcripts.cnn.com/show/lkl/date/2004-08-03/segment/00, accessed May 12, 2025.
6. Nick Vujicic, *Life Without Limits: Inspiration for a Ridiculously Good Life*, rev. ed. (Grand Rapids, MI: WaterBrook, 2010), 97.
7. Vujicic, *Life Without Limits*, 7.
8. William Edward Hartpole Lecky, *History of European Morals: From Augustus to Charlemagne*, 9th ed. (London: Longmans, Green, 1890), 1:467-468. Available at https://www.gutenberg.org/ebooks/39273, accessed January 15, 2025.
9. Polycarp, *Letter to the Philippians*, 5:2, J.B. Lightfoot translation, earlychristianwritings.com/text/polycarp-lightfoot.html, accessed March 27, 2023.
10. Cyprian, "On Mortality," 7:14, *New Advent*, https://newadvent.org/fathers/050707.htm, accessed November 27, 2023.
11. Cyprian, "On Mortality," 7:16.
12. See also 1 Peter 1:7.
13. D.A. Carson, *Basics for Believers: An Exposition of Philippians* (Grand Rapids, MI: Baker Academic, 1996), 23-24. Emphasis original.
14. Another example of suffering caused by Satan persecuting someone is in Luke 13:11-17, where we read that Jesus freed a woman afflicted by a "disabling spirit." Jesus didn't tell her that her sins were forgiven, or "go and sin no more," and He didn't cast out the disabling spirit. Jesus only prayed for her that she would be healed. Also, the Lord allowed Satan to afflict Paul with a "thorn in the flesh" (2 Corinthians 12:7 NASB).
15. Some rabbinical works report that the prophet Isaiah was sawn in two. *The Martyrdom of Isaiah*, Christian Classics Ethereal Library, https://www.ccel.org/c/charles/otpseudepig/martisah.htm, accessed June 26, 2024.
16. Author unknown.
17. A.W. Tozer, *That Incredible Christian: How Heaven's Children Live on Earth* (Chicago, IL: Moody, 1964), 149, Kindle.
18. Tozer, *Incredible Christian*, 149.
19. C.S. Lewis, *The Screwtape Letters* (New York: Macmillan, 1961), 45.

CHAPTER 7—TRUTH 5: WE DON'T KNOW WHAT TOMORROW WILL BRING

1. This section adapted from Pam Farrel, Jean E. Jones, Karla Dornacher, *Discovering Hope in the Psalms* (Eugene, OR: Harvest House, 2017).
2. If you'd like step-by-step instructions for writing your own prayer psalm, see *Discovering Hope in the Psalms* (Harvest House, 2017).

3. Attributed to *Readers Digest*, April 1934. A similar remark, attributed to an anonymous octogenarian, appears in the *Washington Post*, September 11, 1910.

4. Or get sunburned or be humiliated.

5. Chad Williams, *SEAL of God* (Carol Stream, IL: Tyndale, 2012), 119, Kindle.

CHAPTER 8—TRUTH 6: FOCUS ON JESUS AND THE RACE SET BEFORE US

1. Similarly, Fyodor Dostoyevsky challenged, "Try to pose for yourself this task: not to think of a polar bear, and you will see that cursed thing will come to mind every minute." Fyodor Dostoevsky, *Winter Notes on Summer Impressions*, trans. David Patterson (Evanston, IL: Northwestern University, 1988), 49.

2. A reference to adventure-adverse hobbits in J.R.R. Tolkien's *The Lord of the Rings*.

3. The trouble is that if we are in love with this world or if we have other sins in our lives, "I'm coming to You, Jesus!" may not be very encouraging. In fact, for those not walking closely with Jesus, it might be more scary than helpful. A good test might be asking yourself if you wish Jesus were coming back today. If you're hesitant to see Him, then you need to do a fearless moral inventory, repent, and change.

4. Murray J. Harris, *The Second Epistle to the Corinthians*, New International Greek Testament Commentary (Grand Rapids, MI: Eerdmans, 2005), s.v., "4:18," Kindle.

CHAPTER 9—TRUTH 7: WE WILL FOREVER ENJOY A GLORIOUS ETERNITY TOGETHER

1. Because understanding our glorious eternity is essential to our enduring the hardships of this life, we've included some information adapted from Clay's books, *Why Does God Allow Evil?* and *Immortal*.

2. Charles Dickens, *The Old Curiosity Shop* (New York: Heritage Press, 1941), 413.

3. Also, the Bible never says people in heaven will have wings. The idea that people will sprout feathery wings in heaven is an offshoot of the mistake that people become angels. Ironically, the Bible never describes angels as having wings either. Some translations of Daniel 9:21 read that the angel Gabriel "came…in swift flight." The NASB translates the passage more literally, reading that Daniel was in "extreme weariness." Angels are often mistaken for men, which wouldn't happen if they had wings (Hebrews 13:2). Other heavenly creatures have wings, though. For instance, the cherubim in Ezekiel 1 and 10 have four wings, the seraphim in Isaiah 6 have six, and the living creatures in Revelation 4 have six. But none of these could be mistaken for people.

4. *City of Angels*, directed by Brad Silberling (Warner Bros., 1998), closing scene.

5. Timothy Keller, *Walking with God through Pain and Suffering* (New York: Penguin, 2013), 317. There are many different versions of this story on the internet.

6. In addition, John 5:24 assures us, "Truly, truly, I say to you, whoever hears my word and believes him who sent me *has* eternal life. He does not come into judgment, but *has passed* from death to life." Romans 8:10 explains that we're made spiritually alive upon salvation: "If Christ is in you, though the body is dead because of sin, yet the spirit is alive because of righteousness" (NASB).

7. Allan W. Gomes, *40 Questions About Heaven and Hell*, ed., Benjamin L. Merkle (Grand Rapids, MI: Kregel, 2018), 91.

8. For *paradise* as a designation for heaven, see 2 Corinthians 12:2-3 and Revelation 2:7.

9. Theologian Murray J. Harris notes that it's unclear whether the unsaved will appear as disembodied spirits or mere reanimations, as when Jesus raised Lazarus from the dead. Murray J. Harris, *Glimpsing the Future: New Testament Perspectives on Death, Resurrection, Immortality, Eternity, and the Afterlife* (Eugene, OR: Cascade Books, 2024), 20, 107, Kindle.

10. The belief that heaven is in the clouds is widespread. But it comes from a misunderstanding of the five ways the Bible uses the word *heaven.* (1) The **sky**. James 5:18 says "heaven gave rain." That's simply the sky. (2) The **physical cosmos** containing the stars and the planets. Genesis 1:1 reads, "In the beginning, God created the heavens and the earth." That's the universe. (3) As a **figure of speech for "God"** (metonymy). In Mark 11:30, Jesus asks, "Was the baptism of John from heaven or from man?" (4) The **unseen spiritual realm**, where God's throne and all the celestial beings reside. Psalm 11:4 reads, "The LORD's throne is in heaven." (5) The **new heavens and earth**. In Matthew 6:20, Jesus says, "Lay up for yourselves treasures in heaven, where neither moth nor rust destroys and where thieves do not break in and steal."

11. Ann Druyan, "Epilogue," in Carl Sagan, *Billions and Billions: Thoughts on Life and Death at the Brink of the Millennium* (New York: Ballantine, 1997), 271.

12. Here are four additional passages that demonstrate that we will know each other for eternity. In 2 Corinthians 4:14, Paul encourages us that "knowing that he who raised the Lord Jesus will raise us also with Jesus and bring us with you into his presence." In Luke 9:30, 33, Peter recognizes and knows the names of Moses and Elijah while they are talking at the Transfiguration. Revelation 14:13 reads, "Blessed are the dead who die in the Lord…that they may rest from their labors, for their deeds follow them!" How can our deeds follow us if we don't remember anything? Finally, in Matthew 8:11, Jesus says, "I tell you, many will come from east and west and recline at table with Abraham, Isaac, and Jacob in the kingdom of heaven." Are we only going to know who Abraham, Isaac, and Jacob are? Of course not.

13. Mark Twain, *Adventures of Huckleberry Finn* (Norwalk, CT: Heritage, 1968), 15.

14. Dan Snierson, "The Good Place finale: Kristen Bell on the emotional 'tough-love ending,'" *Entertainment Weekly*, January 31, 2020, https://ew.com/tv/2020/01/31/the-good-place-finale-kristen-bell/, accessed September 27, 2024.

15. D.A. Carson says that "although shortened," Jesus' words are an "allusion" to the Daniel passage. D.A. Carson, *Matthew,* The Expositor's Bible Commentary (Grand Rapids, MI: Zondervan, 1984), 327, Kindle. Gomes asks why Jesus wasn't luminous in His post-resurrection body: "Could it be that Jesus veiled the glory of his body specifically for those postresurrection appearances?" Gomes, *40 Questions*, 186. Gomes doesn't answer but I suspect that the answer is yes.

16. Vern S. Poythress, *Theophany: A Biblical Theology of God's Appearing* (Wheaton, IL: Crossway, 2018), 403.

17. Gomes, *40 Questions*, 185.

18. Karon Warren, "Most Valuable Autographs," *Investopedia*, February 27, 2023, https://www.investopedia.com/most-valuable-autographs-5218552, accessed May 9, 2023.

19. Jenny Chang, "10 of the World's Most Expensive Autographs: Whose Signatures Are Now Worth a Fortune?," March 9, 2023, Financesonline, https://financesonline.com/10-of-the-worlds-most-expensive-autographs-whose-signatures-are-now-worth-a-fortune/, accessed May 9, 2023.

20. Frank Sinatra, "Don Rickles Pranks Frank Sinatra," *The Tonight Show Starring Jonny Carson,*

November 12, 1976, https://www.youtube.com/watch?v=q5_V9RT8aR8, accessed July 10, 2023.

21. Paige Patterson, *Revelation*, ed. E. Ray Clendenen, The New American Commentary (Nashville, TN: Broadman and Holman, 2012), 124.

22. For more on different rewards in heaven, see the appendix.

23. Chad Williams, *SEAL of God* (Carol Stream, IL: Tyndale, 2012), 175, Kindle.

24. Williams, *SEAL of God*, 176.

25. Harris, *Second Corinthians*, s. v., "4:18," Kindle.

26. *Focus on the Family Magazine* (Colorado Springs, CO: Focus on the Family, September 2002), 3. Lisa Beamer says that, while speaking to an audience, "The crowd interrupted me with a burst of applause, which I appreciated, but I didn't want anyone to misunderstand the source of my strength. The reason I've been able to do that is not because I'm a strong person. I don't want anyone to go out of here thinking, Wow, she's so strong; look at her! The reason I've chosen to live in hope is because of the heavenly, eternal perspective God has given me. That tells me that fear comes from feeling out of control, and if September 11 has taught us anything, it is that we are never really in control. Todd and I were two people who planned for the future; type A's who had all our ducks in a row. And yet we were not in control on September 11. But hope comes from knowing who is in control. Hope comes from knowing that we have a sovereign, loving God who is in control of every event of our lives...In the book of Jeremiah (29:11) it says that God has a plan for me, a plan to prosper me and not to harm me; a plan to give me a hope and a future. And that is what holds me together every day when I get out of bed in the morning: to know that is true, and it has been proven true in my life to date. It was true on September 11, and it will be true for as many years as God has left for me, and for whatever he has in store for me...and for my children." Lisa Beamer, *Let's Roll!: Ordinary People, Extraordinary Courage* (Carol Stream, IL: Tyndale, 2002), 288-289.

27. Beamer, *Let's Roll!*, 67.

CHAPTER 10—THE EXALTED STATUS OF THE VICTOR

1. Some today object that "sons" is masculine and contend that it should be translated as "children," but it's essential to note that although "sons" is masculine, "bride" and "wife" are unambiguously feminine. The Scripture uses both to explain how we relate to Jesus.

2. Clementine Ford, "Marriage is an inherently misogynistic institution—so why do women agree to it?," *The Guardian*, https://www.theguardian.com/lifeandstyle/2023/oct/31/marriage-is-an-inherently-misogynistic-institution-so-why-do-women-agree-to-it, accessed November 11, 2024.

3. Ford, "Marriage is an inherently misogynistic institution."

4. Luke 12:2-5.

5. Philippians 1:29 NASB: "For to you it has been granted for Christ's sake, not only to believe in Him, but also to suffer on His behalf." About this Richard R. Melick writes, "The words 'on behalf of' appear to be vicarious, i.e., in his place." Richard R. Melick, *Philippians, Colossians, Philemon*, The New American Commentary (Nashville, TN: Broadman and Holman, 1991), 91.

6. Sylvie Corbet and Jeff Schaeffer, "Joy, sadness intertwine at Normandy's D-Day commemorations," *Associated Press News*, June 6, 2022, https://apnews.com/article/france-world-war-ii

-veterans-government-and-politics-fe08e00bd3edb77a2b937829be6f38d8, accessed January 11, 2024.

7. William Penn, *No Cross, No Crown* (1669 pamphlet).

8. C.S. Lewis, *The Lion, the Witch, and the Wardrobe* (New York: Collier/Macmillan, 1970), 74-75.

9. Dallas Willard, *Renovation of the Heart: Putting on the Character of Christ* (Colorado Springs, CO: Navpress, 2002), 51.

10. G.K. Beale, *The Book of Revelation*, New International Greek Testament Commentary (Grand Rapids, MI: Eerdmans, 1999), 209.

11. Grant R. Osborne, *Revelation,* Baker Exegetical Commentary on the New Testament (Grand Rapids, MI: Baker, 2002), 214.

12. Osborne, *Revelation*, 214-215.

13. We're asked, "But what will we reign over?" Adam and Eve were given reign over all the animals on the earth, and I suspect that in the kingdom to come there will be many different kinds of creatures over which we might reign, and we *suspect* that they will all be able to speak.

14. Beale writes, "The bride is also called the Lamb's 'wife,' since betrothal was much more closely related to marriage in biblical culture. Already in 19:7 'wife'...was used as a synonym for 'bride,'...and translated there as 'bride' in most versions." Beale, *Revelation*, 1063.

15. As premillennialist Revelation commentator Grant Osborne puts it: "Is the New Jerusalem the place in which the saints reside, or is it a symbol of the saints themselves? Thusing (1968) says it is not so much a place as the perfected people themselves, and Gundry (1987: 256) argues strongly that 'John is not describing the eternal dwelling place of the saints; he is describing them and them alone.' Thus it describes their future state rather than their future home (see also Draper 1988: 42). Mounce (1998: 382) connects this with 1 Cor. 3:16-17, where the believers are the temple of God; here they are the city of God, visualizing 'the church in its perfected and eternal state.' Yet while it is possible that John transformed the Jewish tradition of an end-time New Jerusalem into a symbol of the people themselves, that is not required by the text... Babylon was both a people and a place, and that is the better answer here. In short, it represents heaven as both the saints who inhabit it and their dwelling place." Osborne, *Revelation,* 733.

16. Osborne, *Revelation,* 671.

17. See also Luke 13:29: "And people will come from east and west, and from north and south, and recline at table in the kingdom of God." Luke 14:16-17: "But he said to him, 'A man once gave a great banquet and invited many. And at the time for the banquet he sent his servant to say to those who had been invited, "Come, for everything is now ready."' " Revelation 3:20: "Behold, I stand at the door and knock. If anyone hears my voice and opens the door, I will come in to him and eat with him, and he with me."

18. In heaven we probably won't be eating animals, but we should expect something better in their place.

19. Beale, *Revelation*, 944.

20. Beale, *Revelation*, 1045.

21. If you'd like to hear the Dixie Cups version of the song, you can find it here: youtube.com/watch?v=rTq7w8P6_2I, accessed May 14, 2025.

22. Rolling Stone, "500 Greatest Songs of All Time (2004)," *Rolling Stone*, December 11, 2003, https://

www.rollingstone.com/music/music-lists/500-greatest-songs-of-all-time-151127/the-dixie-cups-chapel-of-love-54515/, accessed November 11, 2024.

23. Niraj Chokshi, "Joan Marie Johnson, of the Singing Trio the Dixie Cups, Dies at 72," *New York Times*, October 8, 2016, https://www.nytimes.com/2016/10/08/arts/music/joan-marie-johnson-a-founder-of-the-dixie-cups-dies-at-72.html, accessed November 11, 2024.

24. Sadly, because so many people live together today prior to marriage, so much of the former excitement associated with getting married is greatly diminished.

CONCLUSION: VICTORY IN SUFFERING AND ETERNAL GLORY

1. The "second death" is being thrown into the lake of fire (Revelation 20:14).

2. Hebrews 10:34: "For you had compassion on those in prison, and you joyfully accepted the plundering of your property, since you knew that you yourselves had a better possession and an abiding one."

3. G.K. Beale, *The Book of Revelation*, New International Greek Testament Commentary (Grand Rapids, MI: Eerdmans, 1999), 243.

4. Polycarp, *Martyrdom of Polycarp* or *The Letter of the Smyrnaeans*, J.B. Lightfoot, trans., revised into modern English by Richard Neil Shrout, https://www.earlychristianwritings.com/text/polycarp-smyrnaeans.html, 9:2, accessed January 15, 2025.

5. Polycarp, *Martyrdom of Polycarp*, 9:3.

6. Polycarp, *Martyrdom of Polycarp*, 10:1.

7. Polycarp, *Martyrdom of Polycarp*, 14:2-3. We changed "art" to "are" for modern readability.

8. Polycarp, *Martyrdom of Polycarp*, 15:2-16:1.

9. Polycarp, *Letter to the Philippians*, J.B. Lightfoot trans., https://www.earlychristianwritings.com/text/polycarp-lightfoot.html, accessed March 27, 2023, 5:2. Emphasis in original. Perhaps, Polycarp had 2 Timothy 2:12 in mind: "If we endure, we will also reign with him; if we deny him, he also will deny us."

10. Paige Patterson, *Revelation*, ed. E. Ray Clendenen, The New American Commentary (Nashville, TN: Broadman and Holman, 2012), 96.

APPENDIX: ANSWERS TO COMMON QUESTIONS

1. See also Proverbs 11:14: "Where there is no guidance, a people falls, but in an abundance of counselors there is safety."

2. I (Clay) am indebted to my first counseling professor, Dr. Leonard Cerny, for many of these insights.

3. Paul Grimmond, *Suffering Well: The Predictable Surprise of Christian Suffering*, Guidebooks for Life (Kingsford, Australia: Matthias Media, 2012), s.v., "Chapter 1," "Story 2: Suffering and the new morality," Kindle.

4. Grimmond, *Suffering Well*, s.v., "Chapter 7," "Suffering as legitimate children," Kindle.

5. Gordon D. Fee, *The First Epistle to the Corinthians*, The New International Commentary on the New Testament (Grand Rapids, MI: Eerdmans, 1987), 143. Emphasis original.

OTHER HARVEST HOUSE READING BY CLAY AND JEAN E. JONES

BOOKS BY CLAY

If God is good, why is there so much evil in the world? The answer might surprise you. As you take a look at the Bible's response, you'll discover afresh the contrasting abundance of God's grace and the extraordinary destiny of believers.

Clay examines the many ways of facing death and how our "immortality projects" are largely unsuccessful, even destructive. He also points to the hope of the only true immortality available to all.

BOOKS COAUTHORED BY JEAN

Discovering Hope in the Psalms is perfect for group discussion or personal reflection. This study of 10 psalms of hope invites you to discover the incredible design and purpose of inspired Hebrew poetry. Immerse your mind, heart, and soul in the hope flowing through the psalms.

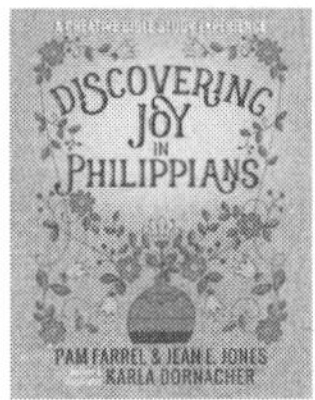

Discovering Joy in Philippians is an in-depth and interactive Bible study that engages your creativity as you study Scripture. This 11-week guide is designed to help you learn from God's Word, apply it to your life, and establish habits that lead to greater joy and peace.

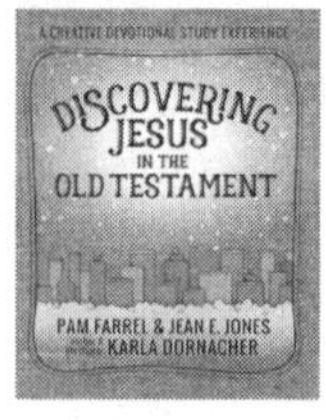

Discovering Jesus in the Old Testament is an in-depth and interactive Bible study that engages your creativity as you trace God's plan of redemption from the beginning. You'll never grow tired of studying Scripture again.

Discovering the Good News in John will help you recognize the profound implications of salvation and see why it matters so much in your own life. This exploration of the Gospel of John is packed with compelling insights, motivating devotions, and plenty of creative ways to engage with the Scripture.

Discovering Wisdom in Proverbs is perfect for using on your own or with a group. This creative interactive Bible study offers you a unique way to immerse your heart in everlasting truth.

To learn more about Harvest House books and to read sample chapters, visit our website:

www.HarvestHousePublishers.com